FROM BETTY
WITH LOVE

J. T. Ducker

FROM
Betty
WITH LOVE

**A love story of the
Second World War**

Webb&Bower
EXETER, ENGLAND

First published in Great Britain in 1985 by
Webb & Bower (Publishers) Limited
9 Colleton Crescent, Exeter, Devon EX2 4BY

Copyright © Bernard Rutter 1985

Production by Nick Facer

Designed by Peter Wrigley

British Library Cataloguing in Publication Data
From Betty with love.
1. World War, 1939–1945——Social aspects——
——Great Britain   2. Great Britain——
Social life and customs——20th century
941.084'092'4   DA566.4

ISBN 0-86350-035-8

Typeset in Great Britain by August Filmsetting, Haydock, St Helens
Printed and bound in Great Britain by Butler & Tanner Ltd, Frome,
Somerset

PUBLISHER'S NOTE

During the war delivery of letters particularly to and from overseas was very bad and often letters were lost. Bernard wrote an air mail letter every day and a letter by sea mail every seventh day. Obviously many of the letters written by Betty and Bernard never reached their destination.

Betty's original spelling and punctuation have been retained throughout. Instances occur in the text when sections of the original letters have been left out. This is indicated by . . . For RAF terms unfamiliar to readers a Glossary is included on page 144.

PRELUDE

The love affair between Leading Aircraftsman Bernard Rutter and a young Aircraftswoman called Betty began sometime in June 1943 at a Royal Air Force Station in Aston Down, Gloucestershire. The war had been going on for four years and for many young people who had joined up the future was uncertain.

Bernard was born in Dulwich, London, and brought up as a devout Catholic. He had a brother and sister, Francis and Winnie. After going to grammar school he trained as an electrical apprentice and eventually became an Electrical Instrument Repairer. He volunteered for service in the RAFVR (Royal Air Force Volunteer Reserve) in December 1941. During his first leave he became engaged to his girl friend Peggy but due to the strain of separation the engagement was brief, and was soon broken off.

In June 1943 he was posted to RAF Aston Down. He enjoyed life. He did some flying, and repaired Spitfires. And then one day he met Betty.

. . .

Bernard's Flight Sergeant had asked him to go over to the B Flight crewroom at Aston Down to do some repairs. When he got to the crewroom he happened to notice a young *WAAF*. 'Hi slim,' he said.

That evening Bernard went to the Church Army Canteen and no sooner had he bought some tea and sandwiches when another *WAAF* came up to him. 'You upset Betty, you know, for saying what you did. She's been crying all evening.'

Betty was sitting in the corner looking very sad. 'I'm sorry,' Bernard said. 'Forget it' she said, 'I was feeling lonely at the time.' Bernard looked at her beautiful eyes. 'Can I get you some tea and wads?' 'Yes, please.'

They sat and chatted and laughed and hardly before they knew what had happened they fell in love.

The following day they went for walks, talked about nature, wild life and books. They had a lot in common and that evening went to the camp cinema but were too engrossed with each other to remember the film. Bernard kissed Betty goodnight. At the *WAAF*'s dance the next week the popular song of the moment 'Frankie and Johnnie were lovers' was renamed 'Bernard and Betty were lovers'.

They became engaged on 25th July, 1943.

This is the true love story told through Betty's letters to Bernard.

Bernard Dean,

Bags of beautiful gen. I went to Shaila (or Shailer or Shaeler or howsoever he doth spell his name) this morning and asked him about my leave and it is O.K. I'll give you the full details of the interview.

I entered his sanctum, with a broken hearted, love-lorn maid sort of look and after a punctilious salute and a fresh, breezy, sort of smile I stated my case to the effect that I was desirous of obtaining 7 days (com)passionate leave and was therefore seeking his assistance in procuring same. He said he thought it could be done but what was my reason. I emitted an audible gulp, and sent an express priority telegram to my sun-god, then keeping my left hand inconspicuously to the rear I told him that my fiance was on leave and embarkation leave at that and I yearned to join him, to feel once more the burning thrill of his (and cut it out). That did it! Of course I could have my leave, definitely so, he'd put it through himself, etc. etc. Well I filled in all the necessary pro forma's and skedaddled across to pay accounts where I enriched myself with a few sheets of pretty blue and white paper and a couple of pretty silver discs with a man's head on one side and a meaningless decoration on the other. (This apparently is known as money and a very 'necessary necessity' in civilisation). I then proceed back to the squadron and have since spent the rest of the day longing for the day whereon I start my leave.

Now I think it would be a good idea at this point to cease meandering off the path of sanity and tell you on what day I arrive at that li'l old backwoods joint, that one horse town London. I leave here on Thursday 22nd July 1943, and go [home.] . . . Then on the 25th Day of the 7th month in this year of our Lord, one thousand nine hundred and forty three (in other words 25.7.43) I leave the home town and proceed forthwith to London. I *hope* to arrive at Paddington at 8 p.m.

I shall do my best to rustle up some 'civvies' and will then be able to 'wear-me-air' loose and flowing. I bet if I am in civvies you do not r ecognise me, what shall we make I'll bet half-a-dollar and the loser buys the winner a pint (of water) (What's that you say old 'bhoy' a nice old porter? Don't mind if I do). Oh dear just as I thought I was getting sane again (what's that you say – same again? don't mind if I do).

. . .

Oh well precious, guess if I write any more I shall not have enough paper left on which to write home, so good bye and don't forget 8 p.m. (or thereabouts) on Paddington Station on Sunday, 25th July *1943.*

all my love,

"li'l Liz"

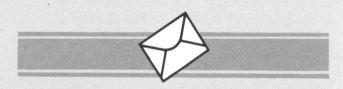

After their leave at home Betty and Bernard returned to Aston Down. Bernard was sent on a special course to RAF Halton and Betty handed him this letter before he left.

My Darling,

If you have done as I asked you will have left this camp by now, but when you have read this letter through I want you to write back straight away and tell me your verdict.

I know this all sounds a bit melo-dramatic and mysterious but I can tell you here a lot of things that I could not tell you straight to your face lest my nerve should fail me.

There is one thing I want you to realise it has taken a lot for me to write this so please do not treat it as a joke.

Another thing, please understand this darling I love you more than I can say and should anything happen between us it would break my heart.

Well here goes with a long and tragic story I think I ought to call it the 'Confessions of the Unintentional Sinner'.

There was once born of unknown parents a baby girl who was fated to suffer through life with a terrible inferiority complex, self-consciousness, and an over-grown imagination. Well this baby girl who was adopted from birth by a certain family grew up but her unfortunate mental complaint, instead of lessening as the years passed, increased, absolutely grew beyond all proportion.

Now along with this was the fact that though her parents were not very well off they had a certain social standing to keep up which was slightly above their means. This meant that the aforesaid girl was constantly meeting people who moved in the upper classes by birth and breading and were not there by necessity.

She went to school with their children, etc. etc. and you can guess how a school girl would feel keeping company with all the local mobs and feeling so inferior and self conscious the whole time. I don't want to give you the impression that she was a snob or that her people were snobs – far from it.

Now another thing that made matters worse was the fact that her grand-mother (since dead) told her that she was different from other children in as much that she had no mother or father and was washed up out of the sea, and that she (the grand-mother) did not see why her son and daughter-in-law should have to look after the child. How the old girl ever found out that the child was not its step mothers own will ever remain a deep mystery.

To continue with my story. Well you can surely understand how this child felt about life, but being the suffer-in-silence martyr-like types she said nothing except at about the age of 5 to question her mother on her birth etc.

Well instead of telling somebody how she felt she gave her imagination full rein and invented for herself a perfect back-ground. Her father became a very well to do gentleman (as no doubt he could be if he did not spend so much money on beer). Her mother remained practically unaltered (she was already perfect anyhow). Her brother and sisters became better than they actually were, she had 2 sisters and one brother. The house they lived in instead of being a nice homely place took to itself new dimensions and became a house worthy of the 'ideal home exhibition' and then to crown it all in stepped the result of a too vivid imagination.

Not having as you might say a real brother of her own, and he not being her ideal of perfect manhood she invented one – an absolutely ideal brother who was well nigh perfect in every detail – tall, dark, handsome, athletic and understanding. Someone to whom she could mentally confide all her troubles who in her imagination, gave her marvellous presents and loved her.

So much for that. To continue. This new family finally became an obsession her old family disappeared from her ken whenever she was away from them and in its place developed this new unbelievably perfect family of her imagination, but underneath it all she was still the same, misunderstood, cowed, self-conscious, nervous child she actually was.

But if you can understand what I mean this practically 'non-existent' family gave her the background she actually lacked and thereby increased her self-confidence.

Being at home though was not so bad it was mainly after she left home and made the fatal mistake of joining the W.A.A.F. that she really found the need for this back-ground, don't ask me why, I don't know that was the way her mind worked. Time travelled on and she passed her 19th birthday still viewing life from the refuge of this mental haven.

Then one day she realised that she was in love, no not with another mental hero but someone whom she adored to the very depths of her soul, someone who was her whole life and the funny thing was he was not at all like her ideal man. He wasn't tall, he wasn't dark and I know he won't be offended if I say he wasn't specially handsome.

Well precisely the moment that she realised she was in love something died within her and something else took life. Just as if her whole past life with all its petty make believe died and a fresh future life was born. (I bet you put the wrong meaning to that). She realised that if she was worthy enough to deserve the love of this man she was good enough to look anyone in the eye or speak to anyone be they King or commoner. She realised that if this man wanted her, no body else had need to.

So one day after a long mental debate she decided to write to this man and make a clean breast of it and trust in his love for forgiveness for all the petty untruths that she had told him before she was reborn.

Well that is the end of my story I do not know the conclusion yet so I cannot tell it to you. I hope it will be a happy ending.

_ _ _ _ _ _ _ _ _ _ _ _

I expect you have guessed by now who this story is about, so I will leave it with you as to whether this story has a sad or happy ending.

Now for the rest of my confession. You remember the night we got engaged, well previous to that night you had mentioned marriage or engagement apparently as a joke but being me I took it that you were serious. Well if you remember on the night you proposed in all seriousness I had been crying now the reason I gave you for crying was only partly true. The main reason was that owing to my various mixtures of complexes I thought I was being pushed on one side again and labelled 'not wanted'. As I mentioned earlier in my letter this was one of my obsessions.

Now about my birth. This is according to Mum. . . .

As far as the law of England goes I am her baby by birth, so says my birth certificate etc. etc. *But*

As far as the Law of Nature goes I am not.

I have an idea what she means, but she told me not to tell you so *do not forget*. You don't know any different than that I am her legal baby. See what I mean.

Now please darlingest don't ever tell a soul what I have told you here and don't ever tell Mumsie or Daddy I have told you or they would never forgive me.

Well darling I will leave it with you, if you find you cannot forgive me I'll understand, but should your love be enough that you can forgive my childish lying all I can say is Thank-you darling.

There is one more thing darling. The girl who lives now is umpteen number per cent better than the one who is gone.

She loves you more.

All my love

Betty.

xxxx

Bernard felt even more enamoured after reading
that letter and when he returned to Aston Down
they spent a happy few weeks together. Before
Bernard was posted to North Africa and Betty to
RAF Annan in Scotland they went on embarkation leave to Bernard's home. This is the
telegram they sent home.

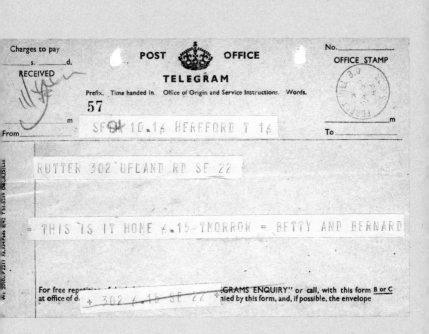

POST OFFICE
TELEGRAM

Charges to pay
s. d.
RECEIVED

No.
OFFICE STAMP

Prefix. Time handed in. Office of Origin and Service Instructions. Words.

57

m

From

SF 10.14 HEREFORD T 14

To

m

RUTTER 302 UPLAND RD SE 22

= THIS IS IT HOME 4.15 TMORROW = BETTY AND BERNARD

For free repetition of ... "GRAMS ENQUIRY" or call, with this form B or C
at office of d... 302 4.15 SE 22 ...nied by this form, and, if possible, the envelope

POST OFFICE

TELEGRAM

OFFICE STAMP

SOUTH LOND
28 SP
45
TELEGRAPH CENTRE

Prefix. Time handed in. Office of Origin and Service Instructions. Words.

67

From   467 5.25 AZT 20   To _____

PRIORITY RUTTER 302 UPLAND RD LONDON SE 22

= COULD NOT MAKE TRAIN ARRIVING 11.10 TONIGHT HOPE

YOU CAN MEET ME = BETTY +

302 SE 2 11.10 AZT +

Their last leave together was the happiest. Bernard saw Betty off at Euston Station and with tears kissed her and waved goodbye as she leant out of the window and the train steamed off. He recalled the words of Francis Tompson:

> She went and left in me the memory
> of all the partings gone
> And partings yet to be

c/o WAAF Guardroom,
RAF Station,
Annan
Dumfrieshire, Scotland

3.10.43

My Darling,

. . .

As you can see from the above address I actually managed to get here safely . . . I got the train at Euston with bags of time to spare, which was lucky, because even though it was empty when I got on, it filled up rapidly towards 10 o'clock. I had a grand window seat and was lovely and comfy until a lady who had designs on being the fat lady of the fair, came and plumped herself down by me, you can guess how full the seat was. Any how we managed some-how so that was O.K. We left prompt to time and set off north. The train only stopped at Rugby, Crewe, Preston and Carlisle, so you can see it was a pretty good train. Isn't the countryside below Carlisle marvellous? . . . For sheer austere beauty and sombre grandeur give me this part of the country, believe me it takes some beating.

There were rapid mountain rivers, marvellous rolling hills, pine forests, wee stone cottages, shaggy sheep, great gaunt castles and countless magpies, peewits, crows etc. even the sky when it changed from a deep Medditterrannean blue, to a dull over-awing grey did not detract any-thing from the landscape. On reading that through I have decided I would make either a travel-agency clerk or a poet. What do you think.

It was about 4.30 and very cold when we arrived in Carlisle and I was very sorry to have to leave the carriage I was in. Especially so when I got into the Annan train. This too was a pretty good train which dumped me on Annan station at about 5 o'clock. My kitbag and case were waiting for me when I got there so I collected these and hopped on to the RAF mail van which left the station at 6 p.m. During the hour I had to wait I went into the town. – The first thing I saw was a London Transport bus – Oh the Irony of it all.

.   .   .

I did bags of knitting on the train, in fact I have finished the part I was doing and am now started on the back. I may get it finished in time for [Jenny's*] birthday even now. I gave Winnie the money for the toothpaste and wool, she is going to get me four more ounces, that will make sixteen ounces altogether. [Jenny] will think the scales are wrong when she weighs herself with this jersey on won't she.

.   .   .

How is your cold my darling, do look after it and your poor eyes too. It wasn't fair that you should have had to go back to camp with such a cold on you.

Write to me soon wont you darling as I am

missing you terribly as I love you so much. Come back to me soon.

We thought of you at about 8 o'clock yesterday morning. I pictured you staggering off the Workmen's bus and saying 'Gug Bordig' to the SP's at the barrier and then eating a breakfast that you could not smell. My poor Angel do you feel very bad or is the Blackpool Air doing you good.

Oh well darling. If I write any more letter I shall have no paper left on which to write home.

All my love,
Betty.
x⋏⋁x.

P.S. Please write to me soon.

* Betty's sister

c/o WAAF Guardroom,
RAF Station
Annan,
Dumfriesshire
Scotland
4.10.43

My Own Darling,

Since writing to you on Saturday and Sunday I feel considerably less cheesed so I expect this letter will not sound so miserable.

I am settling down here OK now and I think I will just about be able to tolerate life without you, it will be a hard task but I will do my best.

I went to the ops room today to see on what watches I will have to work. I found out that I start tomorrow at 7.00 and work until 1 p.m. from then until about 5 p.m. I have free, then we break off again for tea at six and then I go on again until eight o'clock the following morning. After that I do not go on again until 1 p.m. on Thursday, so you can see it will not be too bad. It will be a change anyhow after doing nothing at all for six weeks.

. . .

I went to see the C of E Padre today and I was asking him if there was an R.C. Padre on the camp, apparently there is not a permanent one here but there is a visiting one so the C of E Padre is fixing up an appointment with him for me on Weds afternoon, it was lucky I chose Wednsday as I shall be off duty, it would have been unfortunate had I been working. The C of E Padre seems to have a keen desire to save my soul, do you think it needs saving? You do? Oh well I'd better go and let him save it then as I can't let you get married to a lost soul.

Please write to me soon won't you darling, as I am feeling a bit lonely. Shall I tell you a secret – I love you darling, and boy could I do with a kiss.

.   .   .

Good bye till tomorrow,
All my love,
Betty
xxxx.

P.S. Since last night I have decided I did not write you enough letter so I though I would write a bit more this morning.

I am on duty at the moment but as there is no flying as the weather is so bad I shall have plenty of time for letter writing.

I am sitting in a very small room (about the size of a W.C.) with a green topped table in front of me on this is a 3A Panel a microphone and headset a hand telephone and your photograph along with a logging book and all my paraphanalia (good word that). It is exactly eleven minutes to nine (a.m.)

Alongside me I have an electric heater which is much needed as I got terribly wet this morning when cycling to work you see darling it never stops raining here, in fact the road was so wet this morning that in places the puddles stretched right across to a depth of about six inches, as we cycled along we just had to put on speed lift our feet right off the pedals and hope for the best.

. . .

When are you going to write to me darling one. I wish I could turn the clock forward until the time when you come back again I expect you will put on some weight if you go to the sunny South the boys who go there usually do so I expect you will come back to me looking very fit and brown. Have you had any jabs yet? If you have had any I expect by now that you are staggering around with a shielding hand round your poor arm, a look of agony on your face and a wild look in your eyes. You want to ask them for an anti-cold serum to see if it will help you get rid of your cold. Needless to say I still have my cold.

Have you had your photograph taken for me yet dont forget how I want it done – Profile on but don't pout and if any of these know-all photographers start to make you have it done with a lotus flower in your left ear and a view of Blackpool pier in the background (with a mouse-hole in the South Pier) with your quiff draped artistically over your right eye – Refuse point blanc. You'd feel self consious about the mouse hole and therefore would not look so nice, so don't forget – Profile on or nothing at all (and believe me I don't want 'nothing at all' – the double negative making an affirmative meaning I do want something and you know what that something is).

· · ·

By the way my honey child, can you get them things called flints in Sunny Blackpool? I have tried in the Naafi here and also at the YMCA mobile canteen but I think they must still be at the flint and tinder stage in Scotland as every body gives me a very blank look when I ask for a lighter flint, well any way if you can get me a couple I should greatly appreciate it as my own flint is wearing a bit low. [Betty thought Bernard had been posted to Blackpool but in fact he had been posted to Morecambe before going to North Africa.]

The girls here think it will be possible (when I can afford it) to get into Blackpool to see you. There is a train which leaves Carlisle at one o'clock and takes about 3 hours to get to Blackpool of course it would not give me much time with you but at least I should be able to see you. Or don't you think it would be wise, do you think it would be better not to see you as it would unsettle us both again. Anyhow see what you think.

Have you any idea when you will be going, I don't know whether to hope it won't be long or whether to hope you will be in England for a long time. Of course in the former case you would be back again before you would be if you waited in this country for a long while. O.K.! O.K.! I can't help writing in an Irish strain, it must be that I have Irish ancestors and they have left their mark on me in that way.

I am afraid I shall not be able to write much more to you as I have only three sheets of paper left (Did I here you say Good Show? I did? You bad boy go to the bottom of the class for being rude).

One girl came into the cabin just now, saw your photograph and studied it for a few moments and then decided that you have an honest face. (Gosh and someone or other once said that the camera never lies – or was that a mirror).

Thats not funny old girl, what you deserve is a swift kick in the pants – Bong!!

. . .

I am off duty now but I go on again at six o'clock and I don't come off until eight o'clock tomorrow morning. I expect I shall have written about 50 pages to you by then so don't forget I shall want at least that many back from you.

We have just been detailed to go to a discussion this afternoon at half past two so I guess I'll have to get ready to go now.
Later On
Wow!!! We have just come back from that there discussion meeting. It was about 'Demobilisation' and was conducted by Flt/Lt Singer the signals officer and we were discussing Bevins policy of 'first in first out'.

Never in my life have I been so bored. For one thing the fellow did not know a thing he was talking about and every time some one got one up on him in an argument he would change the subject and whenever someone was stating a point and he got tired of listening he would break in and stop the discussion. Of course you can't have a decent discussion with a man like that can you.

Have just come back from tea – sausages and gravy and bread butter margarine and tea. The one trouble with the food here is that you don't get enough.

Well my own sweet precious darling ('poohey') I guess I'll get some knitting hours in now and finish this letter when I'm on duty so bye bye until six o'clock.

.   .   .

Well I stopped writing this letter for some time while we had a cup of cocoa, after that I read a bit of book did a bit of knitting, etc and now I am sitting with the head-phones on just listening to nothing at all except an occasional crackle it is exactly 22.46 hrs. Linda is going to relieve me at eleven o'clock then I am going to bed until 3 o'clock in the morning. I bet I shall sleep O.K. tomorrow anyhow.

I still have your photograph before me I am sure it is smiling at me. Well darling I guess I am too tired now to write any more so I guess I close down for the night anyhow. I guess you are either bored stiff by now or so tired of reading that your brain (yes the one I knitted for you) just refuses to work any more.

So I'll say goodnight my only darling sleep tight and sweet dreams.

With all my love
Betty
x x

c/o WAAF Guardroom,
RAF Station,
Annan
Dumfriesshire
Scotland
7.10.43

My Own Darling,

This is actually the 3rd letter I have written to you since I got to this dump.

.   .   .

I had the most recent Book Club book today, it is Francis Brett Young's 'A Man about the House' It is one of his that I have not read yet – Have you. I do not know when I shall have time to read it because along with my three-times-per-week letters to you I have Jenny's jumper to finish and at the moment I am reading 'Lady Blanche Farm' by F.P. Keyes. I think it is a book that your mother would like.

.   .   .

I do wish I could see you again. I miss you terribly, but don't feel too miserable will you my precious as the war cannot last for ever and they cannot keep us apart for ever can they? Don't forget every cloud has a silver lining and all that, so just you see that you get a smile back into those lovely eyes again and remember the only consolation I can find – Keep a stiff upper lip and-er-hurruraph – keep your-er-chin up what?

When I came up here first I made up my mind to become a thoroughly bad Waaf, but everybody up here is so sweet that I have decided that life was not so bleak after all and although life without you is wellnigh intolerable I find that I can just about bear it. It is a very hard task though and several times within the passed or past five days I have been tempted to throw the towel in. Oh my darling I do love you so much please come back to me soon.

I told you in one of my letters that I was going to see the R.C. Padre the other day (yesterday to be precise) but when I went to see him he was not available. I think I have deffinately made up my mind to change my religion. The only thing is though I feel at times that I am contemplating a change over because it would mean so much to you and not because I think it is right. Any how I shall be writing home soon and acquainting them with the idea. If however they refuse to consider it I shall either have to openly defy them or wait until I am of age. Please help me to do that which is right. I shall wait until I see the R.C. chaplain before I write home. As soon as I get a reply I will forward it on to you then if they are a bit dubious as to the outcome perhaps you will write to them for me as I should hate having to go dead against them.

Next Day. Well my darling I was too tired last night to finish writing this letter so here I am once more on duty it is 10 minutes passed or past eight (in the morning).

How are you feeling today my angel, don't forget

what I told you yesterday go and get some sick bay hours in.

I'll give you the gen on the town of Annan if you are interested. I have not been in since I came here so I have not seen much as yet, but from what I did see here are my first impressions. It is a town not quite as big as Stroud but the average temperature is 100% higher where the inhabitants are concerned and about 100% lower where the weather is concerned. They sport 1 bus (the L.T.P.B. bus I mentioned in one of my other letters) at the entrance to the town is a salvage dump with a notice which reads '5 m.p.h. through this dump' which I think is rather detrimental to the town. The town hall is in the market place as is usual in these very rural towns (Dulwich is the same is it not) near here is a W.V.S. canteen which is pretty good. They have a 'rorlway' station here which is a cross between Chalford and Stroud and near here is a Y.M.C.A. Canteen which is not so good. There is one cinema known most originally as the 'Picture House', fifteen thousand (approx. there may be more) churches and as far as I could see two public houses. Not a very cheerful prospect is it. Still, I suppose it might be worse.

There are not many means of entertainment on the camp, apart from two Naafi's (1 Waaf, 1 Raf) a cinema and a Y.M.C.A. the cinema and the Y.M. are right at the other end of the camp and therefore practically out of sight, out of mind, and out of reach. The Waaf Naafi is very bad, they have no cigarettes in, very little in the eating line and the only thing they have in abundance are cosmetics, but then as one cannot smoke, eat, or wash clothes or oneself with lipstick and powder we do not find our Naafi very useful.

.   .   .

I had an accident the other day, I was standing by one of those slow combustion stoves when someone brushed against me, to save myself from falling into the fire I put my hand on the nearest thing I could find for support. It happened to be the stove-pipe which believe me was very nearly red hot. I leapt on to my faithful steed and went up to sick bay, where a medical orderly put my hand in a bowl of saline solution. It is nearly better now I have one or two blisters on it but apart from the skin looking very hard and shiny it seems to be O.K.

.   .   .

Do you think there is much chance of you getting any leave whilst in Blackpool. I have found that an S.O.P. here lasts from A.D one day till 23.59 the next, but the beauty is A.D on one of my working days is 8 in the morning so you see it is almost a 48 hr pass.

'Hurry hup' and get your photograph taken for me wont you because I have my wee one, it is standing on my desk at the moment. I always have it where I can see it while I write and work.

Oh well darling my own, I have only one sheet of notepaper left so I guess I shall have to finish.

Please do not be miserable will you darling and
look after your cold.

All my love,
Darling,
Betty.

xxxx
(bags of lipstick)

P.S. I have got a bottle of Brylcream from the Naafi
is it any use to you. If it is I'll post it on to you with
the hope that the bottle does not break.
P.P.S. This is rather personal. I had a shock this week
my pet visitor was a week late before the week was
out I began to have a prick of conscience but he is
here now so that is O.K.
P.P.P.S. I have just dropped my fountain pen, it has
twisted the nib now and the block in front of the nib
has slipped but it seems to write OK. Anyhow I have
written the hole of this page with it so it will be
alright I think.

Love,
Betty

My Darling,

Your letter arrived here this morning and I am terribly disappointed you see darling this is the fifth letter that I have written to you and it hurts me to think you have not received the other four yet. All the same I am terribly happy to receive your letter. It cheered me up when I saw from whom it came, but I was in the doldrums again when I read your first line. It seems as if we are fated not to get each others letters.

I had better repeat in this letter that which I have written in one of my others, i.e. I have definitely decided to become an R.C. I have written home informing them of my impending change to see if I have their full approval. I have written to your parents also to tell them, both of my decision and the fact that I have written to my parents. I hope they will be O.K. and take to the idea at home, only the trouble is that one can never tell what their re-actions will be. As soon as I get their reply I will write to you and either enclose their letter or make a copy of what they say and include it in my next or subsequent letters.

If you want to come up to see me I think the best idea is for you to come only as far as Carlisle and I could come down to meet you. There is not much chance of us finding anywhere to stay in Annan as the town itself is not as big as Stroud and seems to be composed entirely of churches and statues. There are at least three in the market place alone which is about the size of the Waaf parade ground at Aston. All the same I'll get all the gen on registrars, licences, and whatnot in Carlisle only dont go and spring any leaves on me before Friday as I am just about flat broke. As a matter of fact I have just fourpence in my pocket at the moment. So it will be impossible for me to get into Carlisle to make even the enquiries before then. I don't know what chances there are of my getting leave unless I draw a day or so compassionate off next quarters allowance, do you think I could do that Darling, oh gosh wouldn't it be marvellous if we could get married. I hope we can sweet one more than anything else I do.

I have bought for you a bottle of 'Brylcream' if it is any good to you. I'll post it on to you if you think it would get through without the bottle breaking.

I found the enclosed verse in a Woman's Own. I thought it was rather appropriate so I send it to you to see if it will make you feel that life is worth living.

Do you know what my theme tune is these days? – 'You are always in my heart.' Do you remember the one I mean?

You are always in my heart,
Even though you're far away,
I can here the music of that song of
    love I sang with you,

You are always in my heart
And when skies above are grey
I remember that you care and then and
    there the sun breaks through,
Just before I go to sleep
There's a rendezvous I keep
And the dreams I always meet
Help me forget we're far apart
I don't know exactly when, dear,
But I'm sure we'll meet again, dear
And my darling till we do
You are always in my heart.

Aren't they sweet words and do you know? that is just how I feel, believe me my darling you are, always in my heart. I love you so much it hurts. I love you more than anything else on earth and am just existing for the day when you come back to me. I pray every night that that day will not be long now. Still I suppose as the poem says I must not waste time pining for things I do not possess. I promise I'll try to be brave and not upset you by writing of all my worries and troubles.

We were on night duty again last night, we cooked dried egg and chips in margarine, and boy were they good, we must try that next time we are on leave together. I am getting quite an extensive cookery repetoir (is that how you spell that I don't think it is somehow).

I hope you get my other four letters safely as I have asked you some questions which need a reply and I cannot spare the paper to repeat them all so hurry up and write as soon as you get my letters won't you.

I have not been able to see the R.C. chaplain yet as there is not apparently, a permanent one but he is an R.A.F. padre who has three camps to visit he comes here, according to one of the R.C. girls in the hut, on Sunday morning, Wednesday evening and Thursday afternoon and evening anyhow she is going to find out for me which time it would be best for him to see me I work such awkward shifts though that my spare times do not always correspond with his visits. Thursday afternoon or evening would be the best time for me this week but then he may be too busy to see me, so I'll just have to wait and see which time May says he can spare me an odd half hour.

How are your poor eyes my darling? I hope they are better now look after them, dearest, and as I told you in one of my other letters in spite of what I say in the future, except when you have your photograph taken don't you dare let me ever see you without your glasses on, because it is, without doubt, the reason that your eyes are so bad now, is because I was so selfish and idiotic that I was forever persuading you to go without them.

Bags of 'withs' 'withouts' and 'becauses' in that paragraph aren't there.

I do hope you are not moved before you get this letter as I should hate you to think that I do not want to write to you out of sight out of mind sort of thing.

I should have just died if you had not written to me. Thank you darling for writing.

Talking of writing, what do you think of my attempts. It looks a bit ropey at the moment but then this is only my fifth attempt. No that is a fib because I have written two letters home like this so it makes this my seventh try. I must admit I can read it better myself – I dont know what you think – What do you?

You know I am longing yet dreading for the reply to come from the letter I sent home, I felt just the same when I was first faced with the prospect of meeting your parents. It amuses me now to think that two such lovable people could possibly be endowed with the ogre like proportions that my too fertile imagination furnished them with. But then on that day I was dreadfully scared of everything. London appeared to be just a mad town filled with rushing bustling people who crowded themselves into already overloaded buses and trams and careered up and down the under-ground escalators. If you had not been there I should have been in a flat spin. By the time it came for me to leave London via Euston station I was feeling a bit more self confident. I even managed to get the correct tube-train to Euston and got the main line train with bags of time to spare. But then I have told you all that before in one of my other letters so I won't bother to go through the whole rigmarole again. I think I could even manage to find my way safely to Dulwich from Paddington now. Getting good ain't I.

.   .   .

Well I have had my tea, cheese and potato pie and bread butter and jam. Not bad but not enough.

. . .

The film on at the cinema tonight is 'The Man who Came to Dinner' but the camp cinema is too far from the billet so I don't think I shall go to see it. I am getting terribly stay-at-home these days, quite a Cinderella girl although I am one up on her as I have already found my prince . . .

We have been having a bit of excitement here today apparently they are over-run with mice at one of the telephone exchanges. So one of the fellows brought a kitten out there which was very scared owing to the fact that it had been shut up in a sack for some-time. Well when it was let out of its bag it vanished presumably but actually it went down some sort of aperture into some under-ground pipes. From what I can make out they were some sort of disused drains. Well eventually it got tired of being in the drain and tried to get out – like all self-respecting kittens would, well the Waafs on night duty on the exchange thought it was a rat and promptly hurled a telephone directory and a flat iron at it. Much repulsed it ran back into the pipe again. The T/ops there rang up the S.P's who came and stuffed up the drain with rag. This morning someone heard it mewing and realised that such a sound could only be made by a cat. Works and bricks were sent for and it took six men all morning to hack their way through concrete and gravelly soil to a depth of about three feet they finally found the pipe and after a little careful manipulation they finally hauled out a little bedraggled kitten which was half dead with fright. It is O.K. now and still alive and recovering rapidly.

. . .

I am glad to hear that you have been good since I left you. Why don't you go out on a real good booze up, seduce a couple of dames, break a few windows and pinch a few door knockers and I bet my bottom dollar you would feel better.

Bye-bye darling,
All my love,
Betty.

My Dearest Darling.

I feel much happier now that I know you have received at long last, at least some of my letters.

. . .

I do not know what we ought to do about our marriage idea, from what I can read between the lines in your letter I gather that you would prefer to wait either until the cessation of hostilities or at least until you return from abroad. I think that would be wiser in the long run but that is only my brain talking, my heart tells me to do my utmost to get married before you go away from me. I wish Gretna Green was in full working order again, as it is quite close to here, all you need do then is for me to pack my things one night and leave the Waaf compound by means of a silken ladder, you leap on to your faithful nag and meet me at the forge and hey presto! Here comes the bride. What more could we ask for. The only trouble would be I ain't got a silken ladder and you ain't got a faithful nag. If we are going to venture forth into matrimony, though, we shall have to get our heads together pretty soon and come to some settled agreement, Darling. Do you think there is any chance of this happening, or do you think it best for me to rely on my newly knitted brain.

By the way darling, should we get married, would you tell your parents or would you abide by your former decision and keep it a dense dark secret. It is up to you now my sweet, you know what I think about it, My head says 'wait' and my heart says 'go ahead'.

Do you know darling that within the past or passed ten days I have written to you something like 90 odd pages in various letters, and that without counting a twenty eight page epistle that I had written in readiness to send to you at Aston. Not bad what?

Later Well there was a letter from you after all today, but I did not get the expected letter from home.

Thank you very much for having your photographs taken for me. I am dying to see what they are like, when will they be ready? I do hope they will not be long. You say you think the results will be pretty deadly – They can't be Darling because they are you. I thought my photos would be rotten, but they weren't too bad were they. Don't get down hearted I shall like them but what am I going to do with six of them. I'll send one of them to your parents and show them what a bonny little lad they have for a son.

. . .

Flash!!! my clothes are boiling – to the rescue — Well that's half of my boiling done and now for the next half. I have been quite busy tonight and consequently much happier. I just felt in the mood for the busy-ness tonight and I think it did me good as about 7 o'clock I was so miserable I was pretty near tears. I kept reading your letter through and every time I read it I felt more unhappy until finally I wrote a stinking letter home, which I afterwards tore up, I even started on a letter to you which I would have regretted ever afterwards had I sent it and then I hit upon the happy idea of doing some work and getting really busy and hey presto! – result I'm much happier.

Somebody has just asked me if I want some cod liver oil and malt. Perhaps she thinks I look a bit weedy.

I wish you were here darling. I want you tonight, oh gosh I want you so much. This love-making by letter is not very satisfactory is it. I do wish the war was over. Come back soon darling.

By the way darling will you relieve my curiosity and tell me what I have to do to become an R.C. you see I have not been able to see the R.C. father yet and I am getting curioser and curioser.

Well my only sweet darling, it is 5 passed or past eleven at night and I have got to finish my washing, have a wash, say my prayers, pour myself into bed and go to sleep.

So goodnight my Darling,
Keep yourself safe for me,
All my love
Betty.

✗ ✗ ✗ ✗ ✗✗ ✗✗✗✗✗ ✗ ✗✗✗✗✗ ✗

Darling Bernard,

I did notice your change of address and I don't like it. It fills me with a sort of evil forboding, which takes all the brightness out of life and leaves me on the verge of tears. As you can see this is the seventh letter that I have written to you. I hope you get my others O.K. before you go. Please don't ever doubt that I am writing to you come paper shortage, pen pencil or ink shortage I will still find some means wherewith I can write to you.

I have not received your registered mail, but I expect it will be here tomorrow. I am longing for it to come as I do so want your photographs and I bet they are not deadly as you say, anyhow I shall like them because they are of you.

I hope this letter gets to you before you go. Oh my Darling I wish I did not have to think of your going as it makes me feel so unhappy. I wish I could have a jolly good cry then perhaps I should feel better.

Don't apologise for the shortness of your letters, just as long as I know you have not forgotten me I shall be content, and I do understand how you feel about stopping in at night. Get outside all you can and don't stop in writing letters. I am selfish for being unhappy when I see there is no letter from you.

. . .

I had a letter from your father today and I'll copy word for word exactly as he wrote to me re my becoming a R.C. Herewith:-

'Well. Betty, since you are the first to mention the subject let me say at once how glad we are to hear that you are writing to your parents about placing yourself under instruction. I hope they will raise no objection because it is so important and may one day make a tremendous difference to your happiness, and I hope to Bernards. You have seen for yourself that although this is a Catholic household, we do not ram our religion down our visitors throats nor do I think we can be called narrow minded (I wonder what he means there B.???) to continue:-

'I hope for the happiness of yourself and Bernard that you will go under instruction and become convinced; your motive in desiring to become a Catholic must come from conviction, no Priest on top of his job, and most of them are, would receive you into the Church on any other terms. Better a good Protestant than a bad Catholic'

He finishes by saying:-

'You know already that if ever you marry and please God you will, you must be married in a Catholic church and any children of the marriage must be brought up as Catholics. Fancy a mother and her children in any decent family, not being of one mind on so important a matter. Well having said the forgoing I do not intend to refer to it again except in answer to any of your news, or if I can assist you in anyway at your request. I also hope that your parents will not be annoyed or think that we have tried to unduly influence you, it is a matter for your conscience, not something you do merely to please Bernard. Sorry for the sermon.'

Well I think that answers your letter now for my own special news.

.   .   .

Did you get the sprig of white heather that I sent you safely, I can't remember whether it was to Morecambe or Aston that it was sent but I hope you get it finally as it will remind you of the British countryside when you are sweltering in the arid waste of the Sahara, or freezing on the outer-most points of Alaska, but where-ever you are just look at your heather and you will remember that I love you above all other things (human, animal or mineral). Do you remember playing that game when we were travelling from – where was it? . . .

I wrote to you a letter the other day when I was feeling horribly sentimental and filled it with all the lovely reminiscences that I could think of. I did not send it as I thought it would make you feel to home-sick, I am glad I did not send it now as I have come to the conclusion that memories are like National Savings inasmuch as they should be tucked away and not be taken out at any odd moment. What do you think? I wish you were here and then we could for maybe the last time bring our memories out and have a jolly old 'story-swapping-evening'.

.   .   .

Well I told you in one letter that I had a bottle of Brylcream for you but apparently you have not got that letter, anyhow I still have it so if you get this letter before you leave England and you do want this hair-oil will you write back and tell me straight way and I'll see if I can get it to you before your departure.

. . .

Well I can only manage a paltry ten pages again today but my main source of inspiration seems to have run dry.

Bye bye my only Darling look after yourself,

All my love,

Betty.

P.S. Please come back soon Darling, please come back soon. *B*

Annan – Saturday evening
16.10.43

My Own Darling,

Your second letter to me arrived here safely this
dinner time thank you very much for writing one
glimpse of your old familiar fist on an envelope
cheers me up no end.

· · ·

Now for your poor eyes. Oh my darling I did not
know they were as bad as that. Don't you dare ever
let me see you without your glasses on again (except
when you have your photograph taken). I am sure it
was my fault that you did not wear them and I shall
never forgive myself if anything happens to your
lovely eyes. Look after them wont you darling.

I also had a letter from Jenny yesterday. She
seems a bit dubious as to wether or not she will ever
see her jumper. I think she will. I have finished the
right front, the back and am now half-way up the left
front. This leaves me with the two sleeves, and the
collar yet to do. That won't take me long, the rate I
am going. She also sends you her love shall I send
yours back to her. (Pardon the mistake, but my head
is crowded out with ideas that I am writing the next
line before I get to it, if you see what I mean).

· · ·

I have often repeated the old adage – 'Absence makes the heart grow fonder,' but I never thought it would ever be used with reference to myself. Believe me darling I never loved you so much before as I did those few seconds between when I first heard that hateful tram coming and the moment when we gave each other that final kiss before you boarded that loathesome means of transport. Neither have you ever meant so much to me before. I feel absolutely lost without you in the evenings. I pray every night these nights that you will come back to me safely. You see I have decided to reform so I say three prayers every night and do you know I feel better for it. I never felt the same after I had finished saloaming Kashani my Sun-God. So perhaps there is something in religion after all. I always looked on church-goers as a lot of Psalm-singing hypocrites but I don't any more, you see I'm going to take up religion seriously. I thought once I could get along without it but I realise now that the religious man is the happy man so I figured it out this way – if I can't have you I shall adopt your religion and then when you are at your service in Nether Bugomboland you can think to yourself – 'In a couple of moments Betty will be attending a similar service in England', and I hope that that will be a source of inspiration to you.

If I was to give way to my feelings, I would write six pages of 'I love you's' as it is I will keep my feelings under control and only write it once here goes:- Darling, I Love You. (O.K.?)

. . .

Oh well my only sweetest precious darling
(poohey says Bernard). Eef I don' see you some more
'Ello.

All my love, you luscious bunch of cuddle you.

Yours as always
Betty.

xxxxxxx *I did not wipe my*
lipstick off

My Dearest Darling,

Well here I am again, embarked on yet another letter to you, this is my most enjoyable past-time these days.

Have you got my other letters yet? I do hope you have as I hate to think of you not getting any from me.

I had a very queer dream last night I woke up crying. You see I dreamt that I lost two of the stones out of my engagement ring, I had lost them in my bed and I had been frantically searching through my bed to try and find them and when I woke up my bed was in a dickens of a mess.

Thank you so much for the belt and the photographs. I think they are lovely and I love you lots more for having them done for me. I wish I could see you or hear your voice again, Oh darling I do miss you so much. Someone once said time was a great healer, but I don't think time will ever heal the wound that your going has caused me. The only thing that will cure me is to have you with me again . . .

I am wearing my belt at the moment with all my worldly wealth in the purse. When I'm feeling intolerably lonely I'll close my eyes pull it tight and pretend I am in your arms. (Joke).

I am sitting in the Naafi rest room at the moment

and in here there is an ornate fireplace which was presented to the 'Airwomen of R.A.F. Station Annan by the people of Ceylon'.

I think I shall go into Annan tonight as I have not spent a night out of the billet since I came here, I think a night out would do me good, stopping in and moping never benefitted anybody. I nearly went to the camp flicks the other night but I found out at the last moment that it was 'My sister Eileen.' I saw that with you didn't I. I could not have bourne the memories that it would have aroused.

Later I have left the Naafi rest room now and am back in the billet, I have decided to go to the camp flicks tonight instead of Annan and I think the film that is on is 'Happy-go-lucky', I hope it lives up to its title as I feel in the mood for something like that.

I hope you have not left England yet although I expect by the time you get this letter you will be languishing in the torrid heat of Nether-Mogumbo-land with a dark damsel on either knee and a garland of exotic lotus flowers round your neck. I can just see you raising a bottle of ice-cold crystal clear beer – I mean water to your lips and down the contents thereof. Dont ask me where you would get ice-cold water from in the tropics.

I was reading a volume of Tennyson last night and came across my favourite poem 'Break, break, break' Do you know it? I love those last lines but a few that go thus.

> '*The stately ships go on*
> *To their haven under the hill.*

But I long for the touch of that vanished hand
And the sound of the voice that is still'.

Oh gosh only God knows how much I long for that
vanished hand and the sound of a voice that is still,
and to think Shakespeare said 'Parting is such sweet
sorrow'. I do not think he could ever have been
parted from anyone or he would have never said that.
Sweet sorrow? anything but, I should say parting
leaves a raw wound that throbs with greater intensity
every time I think of you. Still what's the sense of
getting morbid over it, thinking cannot alter
circumstances and much as I would like to turn on
the clock about five years, I suppose I must be
philosophical and say what can't be cured must be
endured. (O.K. then Betty, stop making yourself and
Bernard feel unhappy by moaning).
Later still (in fact it is now 10.45) (lights are supposed
to be out by 10.15 but ours are never out before 11 or
12 o'clock).

I have just come back from the camp flicks and
feel better for it. In fact I felt so much better I cycled
back from the cinema singing Happy-go-lucky- 'He
sey moider he sey' and 'Ta ra ra boom deray' so you
can see a night out did me good. I was determined
before I went out, to enjoy myself, so I made my face
up, changed my hair style, and went out with a
determination to forget the sorrows of parting and to
remember that you had had to go to some 'unknown
destination' so as to help make the world a better
place to live in. Pardon the patriotism.

You will be surprised at this, you know how

much I detest swing music, well tonight I heard some that I really enjoyed. It was (of all people) Betty Hutton singing 'He says moider he says every time he kissed' do you know it was like a real good tonic, I do feel so much better, Gee do I feel better.

If only I could have you with me now I should be in my seventh heaven of delight as it is I am only in my fourth but believe me I do feel better. Pardon me harping on the subject but I can't get over it.

. . .

Which reminds me I have signed a pledge within myself. I am determined to write to you at least once per day while you are away. One girl I knew managed it so why shouldn't I. Of course don't expect these 10–20 page affairs every time but I will do my best. I hope, after you have gone it is not long before I hear from you, then I shall know where to start writing air-graphs, air-letters and what not.

. . .

Goodnight my Darling,
God keep you,
All my love,
Betty.
xxxxxxx

Well my only Sweet Darling,

I promised that I would write to you once a day
so here's todays effort.

. . .

What kind of things do you like me to write and
tell you most of all? do you like descriptions of what
I have been, am, and will be doing, or descriptions of
the country or what do you like? I'd hate to think I
was boring you only I do want to write so that you
will have written proof that I love you dearly, and
won't have to rely on your own judgement.

Any how I have told you what I have been – am
– and will be doing so now, trying to be as little
doleful as I can I'll tell you how this part of the
country is looking.

Every where seems to be settling down for
winter. The leaves are turning yellow and brown and
heavy winds are stripping the branches of them. The
autumn colours up here are not half so lovely as at
home, I remember in particular one tree clad hill on
the Monmouth road which about this time of the year
is indeed a sight for sore eyes. Every known
autumnal colour is represented, from a deep russet to
the palest yellow, here and there a copper beech is
tinted with the deep purple that these trees affect, and
interspersed with these are some trees which are still

masses of dark green, it does not sound much in words but often as I have gone passed that tree covered hill I have wished for a technicolour camera so as to make a lasting record of it.

Joan has just been into the cabin and done my hair for me. (The sets have been switched off you see). She has made me look like a glamour queen. I am sure you would like it if you could see it. I have it in a very long roll at the back, anything but two inches off my collar and in three quiffs on top . . . try to imagine a hair style like that on me and then see if you would like it.

.   .   .

To get back to nature, as I was saying the autumnal tints here are not half as lovely as those further south. The predominent colour here is grey.

Grey leaden skies, grey hills in the distance, a grey mist over everything, and a greyish tinge even to the trees and leaves just to be pally, even the huts and places are grey. All the leaves are either a yellowish brown or a dry deffinate brown, the gaunt, bare branches of the trees stretch in a morbid silouhette against the bleak greyness of the sky. Flocks of crows, and rooks with their hopeless cawing cry float about the sky and wee sparrows fluff out their feathers and stand morosely contemplating the grey earth. Not a very cheerful part of Great Britain let me assure you.

Do you think I would make a good novellist? You know the Zane Grey type – He was always very fond of giving vivid descriptions of places. I don't know whether you'd call my descriptions vivid but that is beside the point.

. . .

It is a relief to write without those head-phones continually buzzing in ones ear. After about three hours continuous buzz, buzz, buzz, it begins to pall on me and the ear pieces hurt my ears.

. . .

I am going to get my hair set this afternoon so as to try to convince myself that I can be British and carry on even without you here. It takes a lot of doing my Angel but I think with the help of the other girls I can manage it. The other girls are very sweet and are, so they say, determined to draw me out of myself and make me enjoy life again. I think if all there efforts are as successful as last night was, you will not, as I feared you might, have to come home to a prematurely old fiancee who will tie you tightly to her tunic belt and not let you out of her sight again, but you will find a happy carefree lassie who will greet you in the correct emotional style and trust you with her heart forever more.

. . .

Well I think 9 pages is good enough for today so I'll say bye bye the noo

God keep you Darling
All my love
Betty
x x x

Annan, Sunday night and Monday
morning – on duty –
18.10.43

My Darling,

Here is your daily letter and this is me writing it.

Nothing much happened since writing to you on Sunday morning except that I went to the hairdressers, it has rained continually all day, and I have lost some of my knitting (temporarily I hope).

. . .

I had my hair-do done at three o'clock yesterday afternoon and had to go on duty at six o'clock, for all that the weather cared I need not have bothered to have had it done. It has rained continuously all day not just rained like we had at Aston but absolutely emptied down, I never knew there was so much water in the sky. Well you can imagine what happened to most of my glamorous hair-do. I had my great coat ground-sheet and my hat on, I had both collars up and a scarf on. I think I have saved most of the waves though. Well hair-do's aside let's concentrate on the rain (Why? Well I've got to tell him about something haven't I?) I never in my life before have seen so much rain, and boy is it cold. Much as we wrap up the cold seeps in somewhere. What it will be like when the winter really settles in and we have about six feet of snow to contend with – I dread to think.

. . .

We had egg and chips for supper this evening at about 7.30 and then at about half past ten we had egg and scallops both much appreciated and very enjoyable. Oh Darling I long for the day when I can cook for you.

Talk about absence makes the heart grow fonder, gosh if you stop away too long, I shall be crazy with love for you.

. . .

I was picturing things this evening Darling. I was thinking what an ideal home this tender would make. There are two single-size bunks in here a desk or bench (call it what you will) a cupboard 2 chairs and a table . . . When the heating is really on full it is deliciously warm in here apparently there are double walls with 3″ of cotton wool between, and the three windows make it lovely and light, of course they would need something like a 350 h.p. car to pull them but that is beside the point, if ever we are stuck for a house we can buy an R.T. Tender from the R.A.F. couldn't we?

If you are still in England at the time of receiving this letter please write to me soon Darling. The two days during which I have not had a letter from you seemed like 2 years. I wish they had been two years and then you would soon be coming home to me again. Won't that be a glorious day Darling? Lets just pretend for a few moments that you have all disembarked at some port on the N.E. coast and after stopping there for a few days have been given 'tickets of leave' ration money, and railway warrants. You have sent to me a telegramme 'Arriving Paddington 2.20. Can you get leave and meet me' I'd go dashing round camp binding for fourteen days compassionate leave, and after spending the night in Dulwich I'd present myself on the arrivals platform at Paddington. The seconds would seem like hours the minutes like years, and then – what's that? yes it is, it is your train puffing and panting up to the platform hundreds of Air force blue figures pile off the train, I only want one of them though I'm sure I shall be nervous, I shall be afraid to look in case you are not there. Will you have changed? facially? yes I think so. You will look older and browner and I expect your hair will be even fairer, but what about your feelings for me will they have altered?? That is a question that only you yourself can answer after having been away from me for two years, maybe three. I'll just stand on the platform and wait, hoping, dreading, yearning, and then I'll see you, all the pent up emotions of the past 2? 3? 4? (I hope not) years will give way and then what will I do? rush blindly into your arms? No I think not, even though I love you as I do two years is a long time and I think we will be like two strangers again. Strangers who are sure they have met before and loved before, but strangers for all that, no I don't think I'll rush to you. I think it is most likely that I will just stand tongue-tied, longing to cry with relief that you are home safely again, I'll have a lump in my throat and words will just not come, and then you will see me and you'll stop for a moment and then you will smile. (Darlingest don't you dare smile or I shall break down completely) I'm sure you will smile though and then suddenly I'll know how unutterably lonely the last years have been and how intolerable life will be without you again. But you'll put down your kitbag and rifle and what ever else you are carrying and then the tears will start to come into my eyes and as you take me in your arms Wo! ho! what a cascade. You'll kiss me won't you Darling? we'll stand locked together for a moment and then I'll pick up your great-coat and rifle and you'll shoulder your kit-bag again and we'll make for the tube and then on the top of a tram at the back we'll just whisper sweet nothings to each other and so to Dulwich.

.   .   .

Oh my Darling what a day that will be, talk about joy and laughter and peace ever after. Please, I hope that day comes true soon.

I'm sorry if I have been unusually sentimental and emotional tonight but that is how I am feeling.

I know you will come back to me safely. I pray every night that you will, and I'm sure my prayers will be answered.

Later

I have decided to go to the cinema again tonight it is Errol Flynn in 'They died with their boots on'. The title is very similar to that book you lent me once isn't it. Have you seen this film yet? My last experiment of going out at night was so successful that I have decided to try it again, even though it sounds rather a miserable film.

It has stopped raining now and the sun is shining it is still very cold now.

Well this is the third or fourth day in succession now that I have not heard from you so I expect by now that you are sailing merrily down the West coast of France and a dreaming, oh you darling love, of me, Dreaming of me – etc.

.   .   .

Oh well my Darling I must go and wash my 'mits and fizy' now and give myself a synthetic face.

Aufwedersehn my sweet;
God keep you,
All my love,
Betty.
xxxxx.

P.S. Please write to me soon.

My Darling;

Herewith the daily dope, I hope you finally
receive all these letters that I have been penning to
you all this time, don't forget when you write to me
to put the number of your letter on the outside of the
envelope or whatever it is you use and then I shall
know which to open first should two or three of
them come together.

.   .   .

I stopped in bed until 9.30 this morning and then
I got up and went to the Naafi at 10 o'clock brought
tea and buns back for the girls who had just come off
night duty and then did all my washing, after that I
inspected what damage I did to my bicycle last night.

Of course I have not yet told you what I did last
night have I. Well you see last night one of the girls
here Stewart Murdoch by name (Scots by name and
Scots by nature) and I went to the camp flicks and on
the way back we have to do a sharp left hand turn
well naturally being me I turned too fast. My front
wheel skidded, the break jammed, I nearly came off
and that was that, well I jumped on my bike again
and Wow!!! It was like riding a bike with square
wheels I soon jumped off that, I thought I had
buckled the front wheel but I see this morning that
that is not so but the front tyre is painfully flat, well I

wasn't going to be landed with another split tyre so I took it into the cycle-repair shop to have it seen to. It is very inconvenient not having a bicycle here as the camp is so dispersed it is about a mile from the ops room to the Waaf site by the short cut, but when the road over the runway is closed as it was today this adds on about another mile to walk. Believe me my legs are tired today you know how much I love walking. You know Darling when we are frightfully wealthy and can give up our loft over the stable for a palatial country residence, then we shall have to run at least an Austin seven, or at least buy me a horse.

Wait a moment whilst I light a cigarette – Will you join me?

I was eating beech nuts as I walked to work today. You know what I mean dont you. Let me see if I can recollect any time during which I have introduced you to a Beech nut (and I don't mean chewing gum). They have two shells . . . they are a lovely glossy brown and the nuts taste (that is the kernels) taste like hazel nuts. Do you remember once that I told you that the husk can be painted to make button-holes? If I remember rightly when we were at Aston we went for a walk once to the Crown at Frampton and found some unripe ones along a little dingly dell by the 'rorlway' line. Do you remember? The roads round here are littered with beech nuts, I have never seen so many beech trees before. There is a big copper beech tree very near to where Jenny works. I remember when I was younger – Peace time that is. We used to go over the bridge to get sweet cigarettes and what not from the wee shop opposite

the school I used to be scared stiff at night because
there used to be an old owl who would sit in this tree
at night and his cry was just like a lost soul crying for
release from its cell in Hades.

Talking of birds reminds me there was a dead
thrush on the road this afternoon. He was lying on
his back and all his lovely speckled feathers were
visible, I wonder how he was kill'd because there are
no telegraph wires on that piece of road, and had any
animal had him he would not have been found in one
whole piece. I expect some car or cycle must have hit
him in the dark unless it was a very low flying aircraft hit him as it was quite near the runway. I did
feel sorry for him as he was such a lovely thrush, all
cream and brown and speckly, I bet he had a lovely
voice to.

I saw some wild pansies too, lovely wee yellow
and violet flowers on long stems with pale green
leaves, they always seem to bloom when most of the
other flowers are dead. I'll collect some on my way
back tonight and press them for you – Would you
like that? You can remember England's country side
when you look at them because they flourish in
England too.

. . .

Later (6.10). I got too too busy finally, to
complete this letter, so I had to give it up again,
anyhow I am off duty again now so I can continue
this in peace.

I'm sitting in the hut by the fire, on the end of
somebody elses bed. I shall be going to the Naafi in a

few moments so I shall be able to get a stamp with which to post this letter. By the way Darling are letters to Forces abroad 2½d or 1½d?

I have just seen something that I have never seen before. It is literally raining leaves. The wind is taking them off the trees, blowing them right up high into the air and then letting them fall again. There seems to be a continuous shower of leaves. It is very queer.

.   .   .

I still have that bottle of 'Brylcream'. If you have left the country by now, I think I'll let one of the girls have it as I cannot send it on the boat after you. If you are still in England – Do you want it.

Oh well Darling I have to write to Jenny now and anyhow my source of information has run very low.

All my love Darling
God keep you.
Betty

Good Morning My Darling.

And how is life treating you today?

.   .   .

I did not do my ironing after all last night – I
went over to the Naafi for supper and had scrambled
egg and chips and Prunes and Custard, which was not
bad at all. There is one fault with the food here, you
always leave the cookhouse feeling hungry, hence one
is always tempted to fill out ones belt with Naafi
buns, etc. I have managed not to spend too much on
extras like that but last night I was so hungry that I
could not resist and after looking at the menu and
seeing what was for supper I just could not resist.

By the way Darling I disremember whether or
not I said thankyou for those flints you sent me – if I
did forget I'll say now thank you very much Darling
believe me you have no idea how useful they will be.

.   .   .

Betty Anderson our Cpl has just been in to bring
me my morning cup of coffee I seem to drink a
terrific amount here we usually have two cups of
something on which ever duty we are on except night
duty and then we seem to do nothing else but drink

either tea, coffee or cocoa. Oh, oh, oh, its a loverly war.

. . .

The Y.M.C.A canteen has just been round and I managed to get a bar of Frys cream filled chocolate – Very tasty – very sweet.

By the way I think I forgot to tell you yesterday that I still love you, don't think because I did not say it that I do not love you any more I do now and always shall do. I'll write it twice today to make up for yesterday I love you Darling I *do* love you my sweet.

We had a sing-song last night after I came back from supper. What started it was this – I was making my bed and was humming 'Silent night, Holy night' that inspired one of the girls and she started singing it with me. After that we had 'Hark! the Herald angels sing' followed by 'The first Noel,' 'Good King Wenceleslas' 'While Shepherds watched their flocks by night' 'Come All Ye Faithful' (May gave us this in Latin) after that we went from the sublime to the ridiculous and finished up by singing 3 different songs together I was singing Black Magic with Elsie, Gwen was singing 'Land of my Fathers' in Welsh and three other girls were singing 'Love come back to me'. The high spots of the evening were when May gave us Gounods meditation on Bach (Gounods 'Ave Maria' to you) in Latin and The aria – 'One Fine Day' from 'Madame Butterfly' Not to be outdone Elsie sang Tasselli's Serenata (Like a golden dream) and I gave vent to my feelings by singing 'Rag-time

Cowboy Joe'. Between times we murdered such songs as 'My Reverie' 'Stormy Weather' 'Where are you' 'Brahms Cradle song' 'The Kashmiri love song' 'Me and my gal' and the like. Taken all in all, it was a jolly good show and I think I will make my fortune on the stage yet even if I am only sweeping it.

Jenny tells me 'The Life and Death of Colonel Blimp' is on at home and I see from the local rag that 'Forever and a day' is on there next week. Wish I was home.

Oh well Darling there does not seem to be much else to tell you now so I'll say Goodby until tomorrow.

Goodbye Darling,
God keep you,
All my love,
Betty

My Darling.

I had a reply from home yesterday to the question I asked them – I think the best thing I can do is copy out what they have written here goes:

(Daddy wrote some of this and Mumsie wrote the rest).

After enquiring after my health and expressing relief at my having finally settled down Mumsie continues by saying.

'Now you have asked me a question which I hoped I would never have to answer and you ask us to deal with it as fairly as we always do; I really think it requires plain language, so in my effort to say what I think please don't go off the deep end.

I feel Betty you are contemplating a step you would regret. I know many marriages of mixed religions which are failures for you will always be a *Convert* and that means only one thing – an outsider, you may think you are doing right because Bernard has told you or knows how you would be treated if you don't do as he wishes for I am convinced that is the only reason as you have never told me you had any leanings towards Catholicism. Therefore Betty, for God's sake let your head be uppermost.

There is far more in this subject than can be discussed on paper, so I am asking you, as you asked me, to think before you do anything so silly.

When you are twenty one, you may still feel the same, and by then you may *not* and it will then be too late if you have in the meantime taken any deffinate step.

Daddy is quite in agreement with me when I say – Wait until you are twenty one' Well that's Mumsies letter, Daddy's although very brief runs much along the same lines. He too commences with some general news from home to the effect that Mumsie has gone to see my Grandmother who is seriously ill again. He then says.

'I hope you do not take any far reaching decision before weighing up all that it involves.

There is nothing more I can add to Mummy's note except by saying – 'Wait till you are 21'.

Well there are two replys I'll make no comment on them until I hear from you.

.   .   .

By the way I am re-reading a book called 'Fighter pilot' it is all about The Battle of France as seen through the eyes of a fighter pilot in No 1 Hurricane squadron.

Oh well Bye bye mon cher
All my love Darling
Betty.

My Own Darling,

. . .

On my way to work this morning I became a bird
watcher, I have never seen any place in which there
are so many crows before. One sees great flocks of
them round here in fact there was a flock of them all
round me this morning hence the first sentence in this
paragraph. As I watched these crows I thought how
like a dog-fight of aeroplanes they looked. Wheeling
and circling all over the sky. Here and there two of
them would leave the rest of the flock, just like a
Hurricane on the tail of a Messerschmidt, the leading
one would twist and turn in an effort to escape the
following one and would finally glide along at a
couple of feet above the ground (hedge-hopping) and
make a forced landing on the grass. And don't they
land queerly too, they glide along for a short space,
hover for a split second and then – plump – they just
bounce down on to their feet and fold their wings.

. . .

I hope it is not long now before you get some at
least of my letters and are able to write to me. Don't
try to make any reply to all these epistles that I keep
scrawling will you? unless, of course, I have asked
you any special questions. Do you know Darling I
did not realise when I set out on this one-letter-per-

day venture how difficult it would be for me to do it without having any deffinite letter to answer, but believe me my Darling, come Hell or high water I am determined to see it through until that most joyous of all days when you come back to me again and Please God, that day will not be long in forthcoming.

Do you still love me darling? I bet you don't even remember what I look like this would no doubt be rather difficult as I change the look of my face so often these days what with new hair-styles etc that you would be hard pressed to connect the Waaf who is writing this letter, with the civvy you last saw.

· · ·

Oh well my Darling I really am too tired to concentrate further so I'll say

Bye bye, Darling,
All my love,
Betty.

P.S. God keep you until you return to me.

My Darling,

Where are you? darling, I look in the mail rack every day to see if you have written but there is never anything there. Oh, dear one, I do miss you so much, I hope it will not be long before I hear from you.

.   .   .

Believe it or not (you'd better take an asprin hear or get your smelling salts handy) I went to church this morning and I am going again tonight. They have just started a new idea here – Holy Communion on the Waaf site instead or should I say as well as in the main Station church.

.   .   .

I walked to work again today even though my bicycle is now available. I have decided whenever it is fine and I am on afternoon shift as I am today I will walk, but when I am on night duty, early shift (7.45 a.m.) or it is a wet day, I shall ride, but it is very nice to walk and I must get some practising hours in for when I am married to you Darling.

.   .   .

I went to the Pictures as well yesterday evening – went to see 'Priorities on parade'. Anne Miller the dancer was in it and boy can she dance. You never heard anything like it. Incidentally in the film was a woman-welder who although very feminine out of her job was very tough when she was in it . . . It was not a very good film – definitely escapist – and yet somehow it wasn't as it was about the war. Actually it was about the rise to fame of a small town dance orchestra who got work in an aircraft factory and play swing music during the night shift. They stage a grand show – get a contract – 'Biceps Bessie' persuades them that they are of more use on the factory staff than on Broadway – They agree – The contract is torn up – Alls well that ends well – i.e. Wedding Bells for B.B. and the 'andsome 'ero – O.K.?

I am finding the belt very useful darling. It keeps my money from jingling in my pocket, and that is a sound I cannot bear, Result – I spend it to get rid of it. I am able to save quite a lot on this camp. I have not yet started on my second pound so you can see how good I am getting. I have made up my mind not to save a specified amount each week but to save what I have left out of my fortnights pay at the following pay-day. Then if I do have occasion to spend more one week than the next I shall not have to draw any out. I think that is the better way don't you Darling.

. . .

Well my darling I don't think there is any thing else to tell you except that which you already know, i.e., I love you, so I'll close now and write again tomorrow – all being well.

Bye bye my precious
All my love
Betty

Annan – Monday night – on night duty
27.10.43

My Darling
. . .

Do you know Darling my whole life is wrapped
up in you these days, everything I do or hear or say
or see, I think to myself 'When I write to Bernard
next he'll be interested to hear this' or 'sorry to know
that or that will please him etc.' Please darling don't
ever let there be another girl will you I could not
bear to think that some other woman was sharing
that loft over that stable and looking after you. I
know I don't deserve you, and I know I'm awfully
mean when I go off in those utterly senseless paddies
but that is only my bad side momentarily triumphing
over my good side. You do understand that don't
you darling – even when I am in such a paddy that I
do not speak a word for hours on end, my heart
keeps on telling me to be sensible. I keep knowing all
the while that I love you and I desperately want to
say nice things to you, but while my bad side is in
command, I find it impossible and then you appeal to
my reason and I see sense and then my good-side
triumphs again and I love you more and more. Please
say you understand Darling. Oh I do wish there was
some means by which I could speak to you again,
even for a very short time.

I saw a very queer thing today – you remember I
told you in a previous letter that I had taken to bird-
watching? well today I was watching my main source

of information, i.e. Crows and this is what I saw.

A terrific flock of crows were flying around wheeling and swooping, gliding and landing when suddenly there was a terrific hullabaloo in the middle of the runway, two crows took off in a great hurry and flurry – one was chasing the other, well the pursuer finally caught up with his quarry and attacked him and then he grabbed one of the first crows tail feathers. Meanwhile all the other crows became airbourne and flew around just looking on. As the other flew upwards with the tail feathers in his beak all the others flew round and round in circles under him till he seemed to be at the apex of a cone, during this proceeding the vanquished crow flew off and made a pretty bumpy landing on a fence with his tail plane badly shot about and proceeded to voice his disapproval of the whole business I suspect I was doing some pretty heavy swearing because suddenly the flock all left off adoring and serenading the victorious one and all flew in the direction of the vanquished crow. When last I saw them they were flying neck-and-neck round Tottenham corner although I am inclined to think that, judging by the pace the defeated bird was going, he should have been several lengths ahead at Hammersmith Bridge. Meanwhile the lauded one made a dainty landing on the runway and proceeded to preen himself while he cawed a merry little ditty, unfortunately his voice broke as he hit one high note which rather spoilt the general effect. In all, a very exciting few moments. Of course, like all great aerial combats it was all enacted in far less time than it takes to tell, but if you read it through very quickly you will get the general idea.

By the way Darling I found the following verse in a Women's magazine today. Do you like it. It is called – *Substitute:-*

If you have'nt any oranges – try carrots
If you cannot buy an onion use a leek
We mustn't eat much bread or use potatoes
A substitute for something's found each week!
And as I'm using tape – I've no elastic!
And I'm quite content to mend and to make do
But I'll have to place one little fact on record –
I shall never find a substitute for you
I shall *never* find a substitute for YOU!

Do you like that?

Can you believe this – I have nearly finished Jenny's jersey. I have undone most of it and now I have only one more part to reknit – namely the left front this may be a little tricky as I have decided to put a pocket in it and pockets are never very easy. All the same I think I shall manage.

It is now 20 past nine and I have been cooking chips for supper we also have a tin of herrings from the Cookhouse which I know I shall enjoy in sandwich form at about o o'clock tomorrow morning.

As I have my hand at the moment the light is shining on my engagement ring and it is giving off vivid blue flashes. Now as I move my finger ever so slightly the blue changes to green and green to yellow – yellow to red – red to orange and then back again.

.   .   .

The girl who is on duty with me has brought the

book 'The man in grey' to read whilst on night duty I have been reading a few pages of it but it is written about the same period as 'Beau Masque' so I have stopped reading as I feel in need of a change from demure damsels and Regency bucks. I must remember though to get that book when I have time later on when my mind is no longer remembering 'Beau Masque'.

It is half past four now and as I looked at the clock I was reminded of another day when we were up until about this time but on that day I had been to Aston Down and back walked from Paddington to Victoria and from Rye Lane to Dulwich and sat by Boadicea's statue and listened to Big Ben strike 2 o'clock. I shall never forget that day. It was awful wasn't it Darling?

.   .   .

(P.S. I feel so weary that my eyes are going to sleep on their own.) What couldn't I do now with a large bed preferably a feather one a few yards of shimmery night-dress and you darling. – Don't you get uppity ideas from that last sentence. You would be there only to get the bed warm.

Honestly Darling I feel so tired I just can't concentrate to write further so I'll switch off for the night.

Bye bye my Darling,

All my love,

Betty

x x x x

My Own Precious Darling,

How are you today? I'm fine its a lovely day the sun is shining, birds are singing tis Autumn again tra la la!!

Pardon the frivolity but that is how I am feeling hope you feel the same way. Don't know why I should feel gay though as I have just had one hell of a ticking off from the Sgt i/c R.T.O's in the Ops room, I am faced with another huge pile of washing mending and marking plus a kit inspection, on top of that I am missing you terribly and have had no mail from home. But all the same there is no denying it that I do feel much better. I think the reason is that at last (thanks to one of our Corporals) the attention of the Waaf office has been drawn to the fact that for weeks passed now Signals personnell on the Waaf compound (and especially in Block three) have been unutterably depressed. She has now issued orders that any member of signals so depressed should at once go and see her. Well now that we know that we have been noticed and can get whatever it is worrying us of our chests we are feeling amply better. You know though Darling it is really terrible the state that some of those girls are in. Every night one or other of them breaks down. I haven't yet but I have felt like it. The queer thing too is that it is not always the nervous or temperamental ones who cry either. We have one girl here who is a super-sophisticated London girl who is about 25 and hard as nails. The kind of girl who would crack jokes at her grandmothers funeral, even she was in tears the other night. If something drastic is not done soon the whole lot of us will desert.

.   .   .

I am getting well in to 'The man in grey' now and it is proving very good. I should like to see the film when it comes just to see what kind of job they make of it. With Margaret Lockwood and James Mason in it I should think it will be a jolly good show.

It seems I am fated these days to read old fashioned novels or see old fashioned films as the show on at the Camp cinema tonight is 'Thunderock' with Michael Redgrave which I must deffinately go and see. In fact I hope to go tonight – getting quite a gadabout ain't I.

.   .   .

I wonder when I shall have a letter from you again Darling. I can't bear this awful uncertainty, never knowing where you are, or if you are O.K. Please write me a long letter won't you and tell me everything that has happened to you while you have been away. You won't forget will you.

I don't know whether or not this will interest you but one of the girls here had a telegram yesterday to say that her fiance who was a P. of W. for $2\frac{1}{2}$ years has been repatriated from Germany. Isn't it marvellous for her, she is terribly excited as is only natural on such an occasion.

. . .

Do you remember the Church Army Canteen at Aston Down, that was a pretty good canteen wasn't it. Ach those custard tarts and cream buns, and meat pies, and Blackberry tarts and apple tarts and so on and so forth. It seems amazing that, after all the food I used to eat at Aston, I should have lost as much weight as I did and belive it or not I am still losing weight. I am 10st 2lb half dressed by the scales in the Waaf S.S.Q. by half dressed I mean minus shoes stockings tunic and skirt. We went in for the fun of the thing to weigh ourselves, it is one of those adjustable scales not the penny in the slot affair.

Oh well Darling there does not seem to be much else that I can tell you now and anyhow I have some stockings I must darn ready for kit inspection which I think is one day this week.

Bye bye My Darling
God Bless You.
Yours as ever
Betty

. . .

Annan – Thursday morning 30.10.43
on duty

My Own,

. . .

We have got a wireless set in our hut now, the Waaf officer had it installed for us to see if she could assuage our depression at all. The only thing that could succeed there is to have us all posted to decent camps. Thats if there are any decent ones in this country. Any how it is much better now that we have a wireless set to listen to.

. . .

Later It is now 5.15 p.m. I have been off duty since 1 p.m., and I go back on duty again in a few moments so I shall have time to add a bit more to this letter.

I had a grand letter from Mumsie this afternoon and I feel much better. She sent me another pair of gloves and 2 tablets of toilet soap (Cuticura) Mumsie said she will do her best to make a golly-wog for Bobby, but she doesn't think she will be able to get it done for me until Christmas, so I can give it to him as a Christmas present. I think he will like it don't you. Mumsie makes them so marvellously too, it will be nice and cuddly to take to bed with him won't it.

Mumsie gave me lots of confidential talk about 'luv' too. She says just carry on loving you until you come back and then if I still feel the same – well – it must be 'luv' and I can go ahead as I please.

Personally, she says, she thinks I won't feel the same. She was or thought she was in love several times between the ages of 19–25 yrs. but she soon found the difference when she met Daddy. But I don't think that way. There is only one man in the world for me and he isn't here. Shall I tell you all about him or will you get jealous. You'd love him too if you knew him as I do. He's quiet, thoughtful, considerate, he's got a sense of humour and lovely eyes. I love him, queer thing – he's a Londoner too.

.   .   .

We are listening to the news now (I am once more back in the billet) it is just gone nine o'clock and I have just got back from Naafi.

I don't think there is anything else to say so Bye bye.

All my love, Darling,
Betty

P.S. I hope I hear from you before Nov 19th as that is the last date for sending presents abroad.   *B*

P.S. Just heard Bing Crosby singing this on the wireless.

You'll never know just how much I love you
You'll never know just how much I care
And if I tried
I still couldn't hide

My love for you
Surely you know
'Cos haven't I told you so
A million or more times.
You went away and my heart went with you
I speak your name in my every prayer
If there is some other way to prove that I love you
I swear I don't know how
You'll never know if you don't know now.

I can't write any more as I think I'm going to cry.

P.S. *Next day* Darling I nearly broke my promise to
you today. You see yesterday I had not got a stamp
so I could not post your letter to you. Well I left it
until today and on seeing it I suddenly remembered I
had not written to you today.

Well there has been no news to tell you so it
would not have been worth the twopence halfpenny
would it. Anyhow here is today's contribution.

I am sitting in the hut at the moment in fact I'm
in bed, listening to Music while you Shirk it is half
past ten at night.

I have had bags of luck today. I tuned in the
wireless and heard Doris Arnold and her 'These you
have loved' records. That's the first bit of luck. The
next is I have at long last finished Jenny's jersey this
is a load off my mind although I will miss it to do
while there are slack times at work. Thirdly one of
the girls managed to get 'Wakefield Course' from the
library and she has loaned it to me. This is the only
Whiteoaks book that I have not read. Have you ever

read any of these? If not you ought to they are pretty good.

I put 15/- into National savings today – my first and I hope not last contribution to our future home.

Oh well Darling I shall be on 'Nights' tomorrow so I'll write you a very long letter then.

all my love
Betty

My Angel,

I'm longing to get a letter from you, it is over a fortnight now since I last heard from you and consequently I am feeling rather low spirited, please write to me soon.

We had a 'careless talk' lecture yesterday so don't be surprised if you soon getta letta from me reading thus:

Dear Bernard. I am well still at the same address, and awaiting a letter from you. All my love etc. Heaven forbid that it will ever get to be as drastic as that but one never knows.

.   .   .   .

As I was chopping some wood yesterday I saw a red squirrel watching me. This shook me more than a little as I was unaware that red squirrels lived so far north. He was a perky little chap too with a marvellous tail. He was sitting on a very low branch of a tree washing his face when I first went outside, but he stopped when he saw me. I stood for a moment and looked at him and he stayed there dead still then as I turned round to start chopping he scuttered up the tree to a higher branch and then gazed down again, I finished chopping and turned to see if he was still there. He was. He ran up a bit higher and then turned again, up he went again and the last I saw of him he was peering down at me from between the leaves on the topmost branch of the tree. He was a cute little fellow and I hope to see him again soon.

I did not go to the camp flicks after all last night as the film showing was 'The Silver Fleet' which if you remember we saw together at the Gaumont in Stroud. 'White Cargo' is on tonight but I think I shall go tomorrow as I have a kit inspection tomorrow afternoon and therefore bags of ironing and mending to do tonight. Actually I should have been on duty tomorrow night but the watch lists have all been changed and I am now not on nights until Thursday which as you must admit is a very good show.

I have finished reading 'Wakefields Course' and am now in the middle of 'In this Our Life' by Ellen Glasgow. It is the book from which the film of the same name was taken in which Bette Davies played. So far it does not resemble the film in many ways and I don't think I shall like it. The story is very queerly written. She took 50 pages of book for a general outline of the family and this makes it very boring as she inclines to wander off her subject – (I sound like a literary critic don't I). I did not like the film so perhaps that has predjudiced me against the book.

. . .

One of the girls in the billet had some bananas and lemons sent to her from abroad she was eating one in the billet today. For myself, I only like bananas when they are crushed up in cream with sugar on them.

Do you realise this is my twenty first letter to

you. Perhaps by the time I get to my five hundred and twenty first it will be time for you to come back to England. Let me see now 500 days from now would bring us to March 14th, 1945. Is it possible that I should have to write so many letters with such a near resultant date. Any how roll on 14.3.45 I say.

Do you realise it is but 1 month and 25 days to Christmas. This year has just flown by. I wonder what we will be doing here at Christmas time. Bags of Christmas spirit and what not, already the Naafi manageress has started to make the Naafi look gay with autumnal leaves and things.

. . .

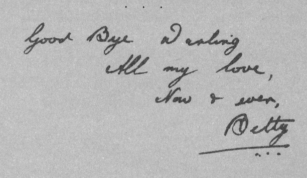

Good Bye Darling
All my love,
Now & ever,
Betty

My Own Darling,

Well I've just had my kit inspection, it was a relief to get it over and done with. I have to go on clothing parade tomorrow to collect a few things that I need changing, namely two pairs of stockings and one pair of gloves. Yes really, believe it or not I am at last going to get my gloves changed. You remember those that Mumsie made for me – well they have been swiped it broke my heart when I realised that they were gone. I wrote home and told Mumsie that they were gone and she sent me some grey ones and she is now knitting me some more.

I had intended going to the camp flicks tonight to see White Cargo no thats wrong it was an Ensa show but I have to get me stockings darned ready for exchange. Gee what a life.

I had a letter from your father today in which he said he was writing to you. He sent me three wee poetry books – Keats, Elizabeth Barret-Browning and a copy of Dryden's fables. They are lovely, and I am terribly pleased with them. I am keeping up quite a long and interesting correspondence with Mr Rutter, its getting a case of 'if I can't have letters from the son I'll have them from the father'.

It is lovely to receive lots of letters although it would be lovelier still could I get some from you again.

They have run out of good cigarettes at the Naafi

again so I will have to start smoking 'Woodies' again,
as I cannot afford 2/4 for cigarettes these days.

. . .

I have nothing to read at the moment having
finished all the books in the billet so I suppose I must
now join the Waaf library which has a pretty good
selection. I was looking the books through the other
day and the first one I picked up was one by Peter
Cheyney (Is that how he spells his name?)

. . .

*God Bless & Keep you darling
All my love now & ever
Betty
xxx x.*

My Dearest Darling.

Well here I am again your luscious bunch of cuddles.

. . .

I got up at six o/c this morning and when I went to breakfast at 7 a.m. the stars wers shining. It was a lovely crisp morning every sound was magnified although there had not been any frost. The sky was very golden and red and I think it will be a nice day today. Not having any windows in my cabin (we have artificial light and air conditioning) I cannot say whether or not the sun is shining. I have an idea it is though as one pilot called and asked another to get out of the suns glare, so unless they were above the clouds I guess it is.

. . .

I bought Polly's Christmas present, or did I tell you. Any how I have bought her a 10/9 box of Elizabeth Arden's face powder and some hair shampoos face creams and what-nots. If I put them all into a pretty box and tie it up in Christmassy paper it should make a nice present shouldn't it?

Ooh I am sitting on a suspender and boy is it giving me hell, Betty our supervising corporal has just brought in my morning cup of coffee. Naafi should be here in a few moments and then I can have some biscuits as well.

. . .

I have my new stockings on today, they are rather nice ones. I think when they have been washed a few times they will go lovely and fine, of course at the moment they look a bit strange as I am used to wearing washed out ones which are very light grey and these are rather dark but a couple of Persil washes and the Persil whiteness will begin to show.

I shall have to give up writing this letter soon as the planes are taking off again and that means work for me – Ah me Bags of Joy . . .

I heard a good crack on the wireless last night, a comedian started talking and then he said 'Pardon my American accent I have just spent three weeks in England'. He was very funny all through and although I did not go out last night I spent a very enjoyable evening listening to him, Vic Sylvester, and earlier on the Brahms violin concerto, played by Eda Handel and the Symphony orchestra conducted by Sir Henry Wood.

Life rolls along pretty much the same here, the days are still light and the nights still dark, the birds still sing, stars shine, everything is the same, the only thing that is wrong – I haven't got you my Darling and that thought hangs like a blight over everything. A sunset is no longer a thing of glory it is just another sunset, trees are just trees and not poems of sheer beauty. A beautiful landscape may be a breath-taking panorama but you are no longer here to enjoy it with me so I see it only as a jumble of trees and fields backed by a couple of hills. Why should nature excel herself in producing all this bounteous beauty when my heart is aching for you, Oh my Darling please come back soon and ease this pain in my heart.

Pardon me for that sudden burst of sentimentality but honestly darling, I do feel so miserable although I try hard not to be.

.   .   .

All my planes have now safely landed so until they take off again I shall have bags of time to write to you again.

The Y.M.C.A. mobile canteen has just been round and I had a couple of biscuits and a bun I suppose 20 minutes to twelve is not really the correct time to indulge in such 'orgies of feasting' especially so with dinner only an hour and a half away but I had an aching void in my tummy which has now been pleasantly filled.

(Have just broken my suspender – 10 minute pause – well that's that mended again).

.   .   .

Oh well Darling there is no more news so I'll finish this letter off when I am on duty tonight, so until then Darling Awfwehdersehn, Ichliebe dich.

.   .   .

All my love
Betty

My Own Darling –

I was so excited yesterday when I received your air-letter. I had begun to think I should never hear from you and then all of a sudden – a letter!

I hope I have your address right as you say you have moved again and for all I know you might still be on the move.

. . .

I have been writing every day since you went away and this is the thirty-second letter that I have written. Will you number your letters Darling so that I can see which letter I have to read first should two or three come together.

. . .

Re those parcels you allege you will send, are you pulling my leg or do you really mean it. Oh gosh Darling if only you do mean it!! Woe betide you if it is only leg pull though I'll have you hung drawn and quartered.

I should love to see you in your shorts. Why not get the old camera out and get some photographing hours in.

Oh well my darling it seems as if I am nearly at the bottom of the page so I'll have to think about closing.

*Bye bye my sweet,
All my love
Betty.*

My Own Darling,

I have just received three of your letters no's. 6. .
and 8. I was terribly glad to get them and very
releived as I get so worried when I do not hear from
you. . . . Now about this political argument of yours.
Poohey. A communist government – my foot. You
may be the kind of chap that would like to go round
sporting a long black cape and a bomb. Where would
your religion be if the Bolshies got their way in this
country. Maybe Stalin has inaugurated a new Russian
church, but how do we know that that is not all talk
and no show. No, no, my dear old darling, let us
remain as we are or why cant we have a democratic
state like the Americans have. Give me Democracy
like that in preference to a Communistic state. You
ask how the news is well heres as much as I know.
(We don't here very much in the backwoodsburg as
newspapers are treasured rarities and even though we
have a wireless set in the hut there is usually too
much noise going on to concentrate on it.) *Item one*
The fifth and eighth armies are still advancing under
stiff opposition and although they have passed Naples
they have not yet reached Rome. I have an idea that
the Red army is still advancing although I cannot say
for sure. The R.A.F. are still bombing the industrial
heart of Germany and I think that is about all. This
hasn't been a very loving letter has it, but believe me

my darling you know how much I love you – more than anything else on earth. Please look after yourself and come back soon. I have not had any further mail from home yet so there is not much else I can tell you. There is one thing though your father sent me a lovely copy of Tennyson's poems. I shall treasure this above all my other books barring, of course, my Bible. I finally had a reply from home re my religion but they advise me to wait until I am 21. They think that by then I shall have found someone else whose religion is mine and who I will love more. They evidently do not know how deep my love for you is. Anyhow I have agreed to wait, I have given you the full text of their reply in a sea mail letter. Paper's getting short so Good bye·and All my love.

Betty

England. 19 November, 1943

My Own Darling;

I am going to give you the reprimanding you so
richly deserve. No you have not offended me in any
way nor have you done anything really wrong, but
you are terribly naughty all the same. For Heavens
sake Darling stop being so cheesed. I know you want
to come back to England and believe me Darling I
want you to come back but please try and be a bit
more cheery. It is difficult I know but the war will
not last for ever, and anyway precious you are
making me feel miserable. I can only offer you one
consolation keep a stiff upper lip-er what?

Now to answer the offending letter . . . You say
you have received no mail from me yet. Well there
are about 36 (this is the 37th) letters on the way to
you most of them are by sea mail but some are these
air-letters. I'm longing to get your parcel, needless to
say it is my tummy which is longing mostly but that
is beside the point.

You say you hope I click for Christmas leave – I
don't. I would rather stop on camp. You see there is
only Mumsie, Daddy and Polly at home these days
and Mumsie and Daddy will be on duty and I expect
Polly will spend most of the day with Babs so it
would not be worth going home would it.

. . .

Oh well darling there does not seem to be much

more paper I still have bags to tell you but that can wait until next time. By the way I wrote you a sea mail letter this morning.

Bye bye my Darling
All my love
Betty.

My Darling,

Herewith the daily dope.

. . .

I have been doing a lot of reading these days and have just finished reading 'Caroline England' by Noel Streatfield. It was not to bad but rather disappointing as when I read a book I like it to leave a lasting impression and I do not think this one will. I expect in a month or so I shall have forgotten that I ever read it.

We had a fresh egg for breakfast this morning. This is a treat that we get about once in six-months up here for the rest of the time we have to make do with dried egg and none of the cooks here know how to prepare it. I could show them, but I expect they would resent my intrusion into their kitchen.

. . .

Do you realise that it is my birthday in less than a fortnight. Gee I feel quite old. Only twelve more months to go and I shall be able to marry you off my own bat so to speak so hurry up and come back as as soon as I am of a marryable age I want to spend as little as my life as possible hopefully waiting.

Now please stop being so unutterably cheesed as it makes me terribly unhappy to get browned off letters from you. Please excuse writing, no more paper so Goodnight.

With love Betty.

My Own Darling,

Thank you for all the letters that I have had from you. They are the bright spots of my week and every day when I go to collect my mail I look forward to getting some from you. Please forgive me if I have sounded rather nagging in my last few letters but I was so miserable when I found out how cheesed you were that I found it well nigh impossible to write cheerfully. Anyhow my darling I'll try to be more of a dutiful fiancee and less of a nagging Waaf in future.

. . .

I have not received your parcel yet but I think of it every-time you write of it and it makes my mouth water already. I'll do my best to get you some penguin books, I know they have bags at home so I'll ask them to look some out and I'll send them on to you.

. . .

I have been busy these last couple of days making a doll and dressing it for the wee daughter of one of the corporals here. I made her out of a pair of ancient silk stockings and dressed her in pink satin undies and floral frock and pink woollen coat bonnet gloves and booties she looked really grand when she was finished. She had long black plaits made from hanks of darning wool and with her wee pink bonnet she looked really natty. I wanted to keep her for myself. The trouble is when the other girls saw her they all wanted one I have orders for more. I wish the girls would try making them for themselves and realise how simple it is.

I wish you were back here again Darling. One of the girls here whose boy friend is in a certain division has just had a telegram to say he is back in England and can she get leave. That is the telegram I am patiently waiting for. Two or three girls have already gone on their re-union leaves. Some folks get all the luck.

Oh well my Darling I guess there is not much news left and paper so I'll just tell you once more that I love you more than anything else on earth and long for you to come back to me.

All my love
Betty

My Own Darling,

I had a lovely surprise today I had an air-letter
from you and a letter from home in which was
enclosed a second air-letter from you. Thank you so
much darling for writing it was lovely getting them
from you. I watch the mails every day in case you
have written and then when one does arrive I am so
excited I open your letter and read it on the way back
from the guardroom.

I have not as yet received the parcel of fruit
though I hope it won't be long. I got the box of Life
savers last Monday and believe me they sure live up
to their names. I eat them on night duty only and I
love them. I gave some to a Canadian girl here and
have now made a friend for life.

. . .

I hope you will forgive the rather dirty air-letter
but one of the girls gave it too me and one must not
look a gift-horse in the kisser.

I wish you were still here darling I miss you
terribly and live only for the day when you return. I
wonder (that is supposing victory day is due shortly)
whether you will be abroad much longer after the
peace has been signed. I wonder what it will be like
on Armistice day. I hope you are here to share the
joys of that day with me. I think what I shall do is

stop in the Waaf until you retun then get my discharge on domestic grounds (AFTER repeat after we are married of course).

. . .

Well here we come to the bottom of the jolly old paper again so I'll just tell you once more that I still love you Darling and close with Bags of love and kisses.

Yours so ever,
Betty.

Christmas Greetings 1943

SENDER'S NAME
AND ADDRESS. Robberg, Revt. Russell B.S. RAF STATION ANNAN.
                                                    DUMFRIES SCOTLAND

My Own Darling,

     Here's wishing you the
happiest Christmas possible under the
circumstances and may it be the
last we have to spend apart.
     Hope I have your address
correctly. There is an air letter following
this air graph. All my love Darling
           Betty.

new year GREETINGS 1944

My Darling,

. . .

I think I have now got over the after effects of last Sunday night's dance and am now quite O.K. again. I must go to another dance soon – with your approval of course.

Have you received the parcel of books that I sent to you yet. I have another one all ready to go, so keep your weather eye open for it.

. . .

Jenny sent me a lovely book for Christmas, it is 'Fanny by Gaslight' by Michael Sadlier and is all well nearly all about the immoralities of the 1870 Londoner. After reading it the state of Piccadilly today fades into insignificance, so you can see it is a pretty hectic book. All the same I liked it.

. . .

I am glad that you are now happier; well I do not know if you are really happier but you sound it when writing.

Oh well, Darlingest I'll close or at least think about closing as I shall not have enough room to tell you how much I love you if I keep on nattering.

I love you as much now as I ever did and I still think that you are sweet.

Bye bye my darling
All my love Betty

My Own Darling,

It seems ages since I last heard from you, what is the matter have you lost interest? a case of out of sight out of mind? – please write soon and long and often Darling or I shall worry myself green. I keep thinking that you are dangerously ill and then I think if you are ill how futile my love must be that it cannot surmount the barriers of impossibility to go to you, so please relieve me of this awful suspense my own Darling and let me have at least a post-card from you. You know how much I love you darling and I don't want to spoil my love by having arguments over a trivial thing like correspondence.

I can almost imagine you saying to yourself when you receive this letter 'I wish that woman would stop nagging. If I do write she says I'm miserable and then she complains when I don't write.' But you do understand dont you Darling.

. . .

Have you had my letter yet in which I said I had taken my LACW's board.* Well I have reason to believe that I have passed. So perhaps by the time you receive this letter, which judging by the time these sea-mail letters take to complete their journey, should arrive in about the middle of next December, I shall be well on the way to surpassing you in rank! That'll be the day when you have to salute me before kissing me!! Bags of joy!!!

* The interview that assessed progress and higher rank was awarded.

Well it is New years eve tonight and the hut is empty except myself and two other girls who are asleep. It is about a quarter to twelve and most of the girls are out at the various dances in the district.

.   .   .

Do you still love me Darling – I do you. That sounds a bit like Mrs. Mopp doesn't it 'Can I do you now sir?' or should I refrain from saying that because it makes you home sick. I'm sorry Darling but it just happened to strike a chord in my memory and I had to remark on the similarity after I had read or written the words.

You know Darling I often wonder if we shall love each other, when you return as much as we did before you went. I do not think I shall ever love you or anyone else as much again as I did those last few moments before you went away from me.

.   .   .

Well my Only sweet precious Darling I'll bid you a fond farewell, as I am nearly asleep where I sit, and close down for the night. I'll write you the usual daily dope again tomorrow.

All my love Darling
Yours as ever
Betty

P.S. My pen has nearly run dry.
P.P.S. It has.

My Darling,

I do hope you get this letter, I have decided to revert back to sea-mail as those Air-letter cards are hopeless as far as reaching you are concerned. Please believe Darlingest that I have been writing every day and I can't understand why some of my letters have not arrived. I have had only about a dozen letters from you since Christmas. Please don't think darling one that my love for you has suffered any serious reversion. This is far from the case and even if I have to write every day for the next forty years I will. I'll do anything to prove to you that my love for you is still as strong as it was the day you went away from me.

. . .

By the way the day before yesterday I forgot to answer two questions that you asked me in a letter I had received. 1) About this bottle of perfume you have sent to me I have not yet received it but if you have registered it I expect it should be here any day now. I still say as I said before, you are a bad boy for wasting money like that, even though I love you more for the thought.

2) You say you have promised some undies french style. Are you allowed to send clothing from where you are? I know one girl who sent her measurements to her husband in Canada for a tweed suit and the letter was returned, any how if you think it will be O.K. here's all the gen on me. (If you ever

find my last measurements I think, on comparing them, I have slimmed down a bit, in fact if I keep on at the rate I am going I shall waste away).

Height 5′9″ (I've grown ½ an inch)
Weight 10 st 10 (4 lbs heavier)
Hips 39″ (I've lost an inch)
Waste sorry I mean
Waist 25″ (2″ gone)
Bust 32″ (2″ gone)
Shoe's size 6½ (1½ sizes less)
Stockings ditto 9½ (1 size less)
Gloves size 6½ (same I still sport my ham-like mits)
Hat size 7¼ (same. I haven't got a swelled head)

Are there any others that you want.

This is not a very inspiring letter but since you won't receive it why worry.

Bye bye my darling
My love as ever
Betty.
xxxx

My Darling,

I still have not heard from you and needless to say I am getting very worried. I hope you have not forgotten that I still exist and that I still like to hear from you once in a while.

I am still writing to you every day but even this does not seem to prompt you to further efforts. Maybe you don't like writing letters, nor do I but I still write them so come on – snap out of your lethargy and get some letter writing hours in.

Something has just occurred to me – I suppose you are not regretting your association with me and finding this the easiest way of giving me the push over because if you are – well I won't say anything until I hear your views on the subject.

Please write to me soon though Darling or I shall go crazy with waiting.

Life is still pretty much the same round here at the moment there is a terrific gale blowing and the rain is beating down on a very desolate countryside. None of the trees have a leaf left on them except of course the evergreens and even they have a bedraggled look. The only birds visible are crows and seagulls and they with their dolorous caws and piteous cries only go to make the scene look even more dismal and forlorn. Every where is damp and dreary and even a brilliant light and warm fire cannot dispel the gloom that settles over the place in the early afternoon. This is a lovely part of the country (Oh yeah?)

I am going to the signals party tomorrow night I do not know whether I shall enjoy myself but I hope I shall as there is not much to do up here and a dull party is as bad as no party at all.

. . .

I wonder what we shall be doing this time next year, I hope by then we shall both have given up this love by letter and are proving to the world that I am not too young to make you a wife.

. . .

I wish you were coming home soon as I long to see you again, it is not fair that you should have had to go from me after I had known you so short a time. I had known you but seven months when you went other girls have had longer than that haven't they.

Do you know Darling I had a horrible dream the other night I dreamed that I had a telegram from your mother to say that you were dead and I had a terrible argument with Francis by long-distance telephone about who should have your hat-badge. He won (that was the horrible part of the dream).

. . .

Oh well Darling I'll close now and get some sleeping hours in as it is just about lights out time.

So Bye bye
Love,
Betty

P.S. If you don't write soon I'll divorce you.

Note: During the War many letters never reached their final destination.

My Darling,

This is the first air letter I have written for about a week although I had made up for this omission by writing bags of sea-mail.

. : .

There is one thing I want to ask you Darling, I hope you won't take this in the wrong way but please do not mention religion in your letters to me again. A girl can stand so much but after that something has to give way and I do not want it to be my love for you. I have tried and am still trying to understand and appreciate the Catholic view point so please respect my request and leave me to my own thoughts and arguments. 'Nuff Said?'

I hope you can understand this letter, but I am sitting on the end of my bed – near the fire and everybody is nattering and singing and begging my pardon as they brush passed my feet.

I have not heard from you for sometime now and I am very worried, are you all right and well please write soon or cable and relieve me.

Have you received the books yet, I am still collecting more, I bind everybody for them and I am afraid I have made myself quite unpopular all round by continually requesting.

A small library here is closing down and selling all their books off at a 1/- each. I think I'll go in and see if I can pick up any bargains.

Bye by Darling I still love you lots and lots.

Betty

My Own Darling,

Another day gone and still no word from you. Wakey wakey. Please write to me soon. Darling I can't live on memories for ever I like to have an occasional word from you even if you write it on the back of a palm leaf with a pin.

We have been hearing some awe inspiring tales lately of fifteen foot snow drifts and confinement to camp for three weeks living on Bully beef and stew and no mail owing to blocked roads etc. Well yesterday we watched the Annan weather doing its worst. All the know alls kept gazing at the sky and muttering things like 'Here it comes' or 'Get ready to tighten your belts' or 'You have had your leave girls' and such like. Well we gazed expectantly at the sky and waited. It was beastly cold, absolutely deadly and we just watched and waited, crouching over the fire and expecting any minute to find ourselves blocked in the hut with a huge snow drift. Then came the snow – all 3 flakes and by the end of about 5 minutes it was finished there wasnt even enough to cover all the ground – 15' snow drifts my foot.

By the way I put my props* up yesterday so I won't stand any more of the 'superior rank stuff' from you. If they give me any more stuff to put on my right arm it will be weighed down. I have an eagle, an 'A', my sparks and props. I only want a

*Represents a badge of rank i.e. Leading Aircraftswoman.

G.C. and a couple of wound stripes and I shall be O.K. Still they all help to keep me warm.

Please forgive the way I keep harping on the cold but it is the one topic of conversation here these days. Perhaps when the days get a bit warmer I shall not have such a crabby outlook on life and will stop binding you every time I fail to hear from you.

I dreamed about you last night Darling – And woke up crying. (Ha! ha!)

Bye bye my Own Sweet one I still love you as much as ever.

God bless you
Betty.

My Own Darling,

Here I am again still writing in hope that one day you might receive a letter from me. I don't know why I keep writing unless it is that I feel inside me that one day in the not so far off future you might by some miracle receive a letter from me.

.   .   .

Well I think it is Monday today so in accordance with my usual routine I'll tell you how England or to be more appropriate Scotland is looking. As I went into Dumfries to meet Ken on Saturday I saw all those fuzzy-buds were sprouting and here and there, there is a faint tinge of green on the Hawthorn hedges a sure sign of Spring. We have been having some lovely weather although today it is very far from nice. The sun has been shining and the sky like a sapphire. I forgot to tell you but a few days ago I was energetic enough to get some gardening hours in. I intend to plant some nice bright nasturtiums on the piece of ground that I have dug. It should look fine when all the flowers are out. There is one thing missing though Darling, you are not here to share the lovely weather with me.

By the way I received another parcel of

newspapers from you the other day. Thank you Darling.

. . .

I am going on leave on May 4th and shall be going down to London first as I did last time but I told you that yesterday didn't I.

I started another R.A.F. doll today, if you ever receive my other letters you will remember I told you about the first doll I made about 20 or so letters back. This one will be dressed in battledress though so he won't look so spectacular as the first one I made. It is a pity but I have not got the patience to make another wearing a tunic and any-how I don't like making two dolls alike.

By the way I have a bone to pick with you you old crow. Whats the big idea of heading your letters 'My Dear Betty' these days. Once upon a time I was your Darling but it seems I have slipped somewhere in your esteem. Don't think I hate the repetition of reading my Darling, every time, I don't. I love it. Please Darlingest don't start cooling off now or it'll break me bloomin' heart, so cut out the My Dear stunt it makes you sound as if you are about 50 instead of about how much? 26?

Did you ever receive those books I sent to you Angel Puss. Knowing the mails these days I shouldn't be at all surprised if you haven't. Anyhow I scout around and see if I can't get you some more.

I can't think of any more to say today so I'll switch off my flow of news before my accs* run down.

Bye Bye. you luscious bunch af cuddl.
I still love you
Your own
Betty
xxxx

* Accumulators (batteries) – the power used for the wireless Betty was operating.

My Darling,

You wont have received yet the letters I have written for the passed (or past) five days as they are sea mail letters.

I hope you are getting my mail more regularly now, I keep on writing and writing but there does not seem to be any sense in it if you are not receiving them.

I spent a lovely day in Annan today with Pat Robertson (she is one of our R.T.O.s and I expect you will hear me mention her name quite often as her husband has just been posted and we are together quite a lot these days). We left camp at about 10 o/c and cycled into town we had half an hour to wait before the cafe opened so we went to the Public Library and joined that. After having coffee and cakes at the cafe we went on a small shopping expedition, and then went for a long walk along the banks of the river Annan we sat on Pats greatcoat and read our books, watched 4 small boys playing Tarzan in some trees and a man fly-fishing for trout – he got his line caught once and had to break it to release it (Spare the rod and spoil the line – see?). Then we hunted for pretty pebbles on the beach and skimmed flat stones to see who could make the stone bounce most before it sank. We strolled back along the bank and then visited the W.V.S. canteen for tea. Pat had to go to S.Q. for treatment at 5.30 so we cycled slowly back to camp. The sun was lovely and warm and the birds were singing themselves hoarse in the trees around. I am back at the billet now and I am feeling rather tired. I wish you could have been with me, although I doubt I should not have been back in the billet and I am too tired to stay out later.

I have not heard from you for about a week or more now. I hope the mails are not going to turn out the same as at your end.

Well I'm getting short of space so I'll just say I love you darling

Bye bye

All my love.

Betty

My Darling.

Not much water has flowed under the proverbial bridge since I last wrote to you but it has been too much for my liking.

I am on duty this afternoon and as I have these few moments to spare I thought I would write to you.

I shall be posting your birthday parcel on to you soon, that is either tomorrow or the day after. I am sorry I could not send it in time for the actual day but I had not finished it in time. I was still doing my kid-sisters and her birthday was last January. I intend to have my photograph done one of these days. I shall be done in uniform but I won't roll my hair up to tightly I know how you hate that. Incidentally my hair is so long now that it can be tied in a bow under my chin. By the time you come back I need not wear any clothes as my hair will be long enough to cover me up. Lady Godiva's hair will be considered an Eton crop when they see mine.

. . .

By the way in one letter you wrote some time ago you mentioned you were having nightmares about me. I don't like the sound of this at all. I can't help my face but there is no need for you to let it prey on your mind. . . . If it is my figure that worries you, believe me old timer it worries me too, a good cure for that is to go drape your eyes on one or more of the local sheiks dancing girls, you'll soon forget me altogether and presto chango no more night mares. If of course it is the fact that you are not receiving my mail then go and 'moider' a couple of the Post office boys and then go and poke old Adolph on the snoot, maybe then you will get some of my mail.

Please excuse this dippy letter but I am reading a book on the P.G. Wodehouse lines and it is affecting my sanity.

. . .

Bye Bye my precious Darling, God Bless you I love you, I love you –

Betty

My Darling,

I suppose it is my turn to get panicky now as I have not heard from you for so long. I shall not worry unduly though as I know you are writing to me.

I had an evening out last night. Two other girls and I cycled into Annan. We went first into the W.V.S. Services canteen for a coffee and a bun and then made our way to the Picture House. We hadn't the faintest idea what was on and when we got there all the seats were taken except a few nine-pennies. We decided in favour of these as otherwise we should have had to stand. There was a cartoon on when we went in and as you know when you go in in the middle of those things they don't mean much or make much sense. Our seats were right in the front row and we had to be gazing upwards all the time. After the cartoon was a film about a dog and was very good. Then came the big picture. We still did not recognise it as we could not read the Board of Entertainment Certificate as we were craning our necks too hard as it was. Ultimately it turned out to be 'Hold back the Dawn' and was very enjoyable. It would have been more so had we been able to see properly.

When we came out I had been gazing skywards for so long that it was painful to put my head down. I still feel a faint click in the back of my neck when I look up or down now.

By the way darling I intended saying in yesterdays letter about what colour handbag I would like. I should like a blue, black or brown one. If they haven't any of those colours, any colour will do. You are a precious Angel thinking of me like that I love you lots for it.

Spring is deffinately in the air now, although today isn't so good. Theres bags of green everywhere and the birds are singing like mad. I wish that——no I mustn't keep wishing you were here or you'll be getting dissatisfied.

One of the girls in the hut got her discharge today on domestic reasons. Some folks have all the luck. If this war doesn't end soon I think I'll spend a slightly soiled S.O.P. with the nearest man and get out that way. Would you mind bringing up some-one else's child?

Bye Bye Darling
All my love
Betty.

My Darling,

. . .

I am on duty this afternoon and it is a lovely day, blue sky, birds singing, bags of sunshine and very warm. It is the type of day Browning was thinking of when he cried 'Oh to be in England now that April's here' except that this is May and not April.

There is a flock of sheep here and we have watched the lambs from babyhood they are getting quite large now. I expect they will soon be gracing somebodies table as mutton or lamb chops. Among the flock are four pure black lambs they look like rather woolly panthers.

I had a leter from Daddy the other day he says he has started an asparagus bed so when you return home again there may be some grown enough to eat. It takes a hell of a time to grow.

I sent Mumsies table cloth off the other day. She said it arrived on May the fourth the 24th (I think) anniversary of her wedding. I had intended it for her birthday but circumstances interfered so that I was 2 months all but 2 days late. I never could be punctual could I. I remember once I was so late I had only ten minutes to wait for you (sarcasm).

By now you should have received the air-letter in which I said I had received the perfume, and now I am longing for the hand-bag undies and my 21st Birthday to roll around. Many thanks Darling, you're sweet.

. . .

By the way do you ever here the General Forces programme on the wireless. I listen to it pretty regularly especially to Doris Arnold's 'These you have loved' and to Margory Whatsernames programmes of classical pieces. When we are married we must treat ourselves to a gramophone and then supply ourselves with a collection of all my favourite records. (I might allow you to have a few of your favourites too if you are a good boy).

Eric, Sheila, Anthony, Carol, Stephen, Christina and Baby's Paul and Elaine all send their love and want to know when you are coming home.* Paul can now say Dadda but Elaine sticks to Mamma. Eric says don't forget to bring him a camel and Sheila wants some dates (she did not specify which sort).

There does not seem to be much space left for anything else so I'll get some closing down hours in.

Love from all eight of the kids.

Yours for ever darling
Your Wife (to-be)
Betty xxx

---

*Betty fantasised about the family they were going to have when Bernard came home.

Darling,

Please pardon the blots at the top my pen was over-full. By now you will have had my letter wherein I said I had changed my address, if you have not my address is now 'Receiver Site' or just 'Receivers' R.A.F. Annan.

I am very happy up here and service life does not seem half so bad. The cynic in me though keeps telling me it is too good to last but I hope I can stay here. I think I'll have a jaunt into Carlisle this afternoon as there is a good film on – Spencer Tracey in 'A Guy named Joe'. There is one thing about this place I bet I shall be able to save a bit more cash than I could on the camp. It was hopeless to try there although I have got a bit put by for that day of days when we decide to make a go of married life. Wont that be a lovely day can you imagine me as a demure and blushing bride. I realise that is absolutely asking for a dirty crack but you needn't bother as I have them all worked out.

It is a lovely day today quite a change from the weather we have had, it has been more like January than June, but today it is getting a better idea of what a June day should be like and I hope the fine weather has come to stay now, then I can get some more swimming hours in. Which reminds me I am very pleased to here that you are now able to float a little keep up the good work and one day I shall have you challenging Johnny Weissmuller as the future World Champion.

All the children send their love and hope that it is not going to be too long before you are home again. That goes for me too in a very big way. This war cannot last for ever so one day – one very glad day you will be on a ship labelled 'England with love' and then Oh Joy of joys I'll see you agan.

Bye bye Darling
all love
Betty

My Darling,

I had a lovely surprise today, I received a parcel from home it was about 6″ by 6″ by 6″ and showed signs of much travel, it had a wee tin seal on it marked O.S. and looked frightfully official. There were a couple of censors labels on it and my name and address were written in a vaguely familiar hand writing as well as these someone else (Polly I think) had stuck two more labels on to address it. I feverishly tore off the paper and string and found myself confronted by a square wooden box. This flummoxed me more than somewhat as the G.P.O. or the censor had made a very good job of re-sealing it. Nothing daunted I proceeded to heave off the outer shell only to find a layer of paper shavings, scattering this I delved into the depths and drew forth a wee parcel of corrugated cardboard. This was beginning to pall on me as it seemed to be developping into one of those Christmas parcel games I persevered though and removed the card-board. By this time a most heavenly smell was penetrating my senses and as I removed the last layer of card-board I was confronted by a little brown bottle, with the word Integral (I forget whether the accent should be acute or abtuse). Oh Darling it is a lovely, divine, marvellous, perfectly delightful delovely. The girls and I have decided to call it 'Blackout Passion', 'Brazilian Night' 'Naught naughty' or 'Passionate Surrender'. Thank you lots and lots Darling. Geez when we are married I'll stink the house out and Sheila, Carol and Christina shall each have some when they go to their first dances.

That rhyme you sent me was most crude and deffinately bad taste, I wish you weren't like that. Do you realise that no matter what I do or say you always put another meaning to it and usually a sexy one. Consider yourself wallopped by post.

. . .

Bye bye Darling
all love
Betty . xxxx

Receivers Section,
RAF Station,
Annan,
Dumfriesshire.
18.6.44

Darling One,

Yesterday was Derby day and I have just been
listening to Sports Gazette and with it a recorded
version of the running of the Derby. I bet it was a
close finish – I won 3/6 (4/- counting my own tanner)
on Ocean Swell so now I am feeling quite good
towards the owner trainer and jockey. I also had
threepence on Gordon Path, but she failed me. At the
moment I am listening to Palace of Variety, and a girl
singing 'Give my regards to Leicester Square dear
Piccadilly and Mayfair, mention me to the folks
round there they'll understand.' Speaking of that –
Leicester Square and whatnot, when shall I be
walking down Bond Street or Victoria Street (ugh!
do you remember) with you again. I think you have
been away quite long enough so I think I'll write to
Sir Charles Portal* and tell him so. I wonder what he
would say in reply – if he replied. I expect I should
be bunged on a charge for addressing my superior
officer through the unusual channells.

Yesterday I went to Carlisle and met a Flt-Lt (pre
Ops type) but as I came back in the bus with him I
kept trying to pretend he was you, and it just

*Marshal of the Royal Air Force.

wouldn't work. I just felt awfully moody, so I am afraid he did not think me a very entertaining companion. Anyhow, he wants to take me to see 'Desert Song' next Wednesday but I don't think I shall go. Don't think that I am growing away from you because I go out with him. I'm not. Only a girl cant stop in for ever can she and no man has kissed me since you went away and Don thats this Peelo type understands about you and he says he has a fiancee of his own back in New Zealand so we are just keeping each other company. But I still wish that you were here instead he may be tall dark and so-so looking as well as being an aircrew officer type, I prefer my blonde Lac instr-rep. Still he is very nice and does as a stand-in until said B: LAC. R. comes back.

Jenny suggested in a letter today that you would be mad, not being in this Second Front – Are you? You 'adn't better. I prefer you out there and fairly safe rather than stuck on a beach in Northern France changing Oxygen bottles in Spitfires while bullets whiz around. No sirree. Either you come back to England (but don't get torpedoed on the way or killed by a peelo-less plane when you get here) or stop where you are.

You mentioned in one letter that I still have not told you whether I should like some silver jewellery for my 21st. Actually I have written in several letters both – Thanks for the lovely handbag and also I should love some silver jewellery, but you must not buy me any as I think you spend too much money on me and we shall never have enough for our post war

home and I don't fancy rearing a family on nothing.
Do you see what I mean. Please don't think me
ungrateful, actually the vanity in me nearly breaks its
heart to read what I have written above but – Oh
gosh why do I always tie myself in such a knot when
trying to explain anything and why do I always have
to play Miss Kiljoy. Look darling – if it gives you
pleasure to make me happy – I do not mind being
made happy at all – in fact I love it.

19.6.44

I have just been listening to the news isn't it
great. We've cut the Cherbourg Peninsular and
attacked somewhere. Your marvellous Red Army has
now got as far as Vipurie (I think thats right). The
Pacific War is going O.K. and we are now 82 miles
N.E. of Rome. What a war – 5 years after the start
and we start wakening up and doing things.

Oh well Darling. If I do not finish this letter soon
I shall be getting told off for holding up the mails.

Bye-bye darling,
All my love,
Betty.

Dear One,

Still no mail from you. Another week and I shall start really panicing. Why Oh why can't somebody think of a way of getting mail to North Africa and back quickly and efficiently. It isn't fair that we here at home should have to sit day in day out wondering, waiting, and longing for mail to come. Ah well C'est le guerre.

. . .

Nothing of importance has happened since I wrote to you yesterday except that earlier this morning while I was on duty I had a surprise visit from our new Groupy. He got quite ugly because I asked him for his twelve fifty and wouldn't let him into the section until I had seen it. While he was there he asked me to show him how a set was tuned. Of course the damned thing wouldn't work. Isn't it always the way.

How is Marie, please give her my kindest regards – her name is Marie isn't it or have you found someone else who you like better whose mother has a larger table for you to get your feet under and a more ample supply of food for you to tuck into (Bit o' good grammar that).

I have just finished reading a most amazing book about a Jewish family in Germany between the years 1929 and 1939. How much of it is true I do not know but it is really a terrific book. I am just about to start reading Gibbons, Christianity or Christianity through the ages. I can't remember the actual title but I think, although it will be rather deep, I shall find it sufficiently interesting to keep me entertained for a few days.

Did I tell you that I finally got the centre stone of my engagement ring tightened.

I am very short of news today am I not all the same I intend to visit Annan this afternoon so I shall be able to tell you about that in tomorrows letter.

Bye Bye & Keep smiling
Heah lookin' at you Kid.
Betty

My Own Darling,

This is the fifth letter I have written since I received yours in which you asked me about the little watch that you can get and as I've said in the others I should love it – if and it is an important 'if' – it is not going to cost too much. On no account are you to even contemplate buying it if it means that you have got to lay out pounds and pounds.

.   .   .

I have just finished reading for the second time Dennis Wheatley 'Strange Conflict' and am now engrossed in a most interesting book Leslie D. Weatherhead's 'Mastery of Sex' it is a frank and fearless book and beautifully written.

It is terribly muggily hot today and as I was coming up from Annan I was over-whelmed with flies, Big grey ones that bite like mad.

At the moment (that is before I started this letter) I am busy sewing lace onto a dolls petticoat, this is about the 31st or 32nd doll I have made since last December. It is surprising how interesting they are to do. I think I had better make a Waaf Doll and send it to you.

Have you yet received any of the other books and map that I have sent and is there anything that you specially need that I can get for you?

Shall have to cease now as I have no more room.

Lots of love   Betty xxx

Suddenly the letters stopped.
Then Bernard heard from Betty's parents:

Dear Bernard,

   We regret to have to tell you that Betty was killed on Active Service in Annan 10:7:44.

   May God comfort us all in our Great Loss.

                    Affectionately.

Before leaving Tunis Bernard received this last letter.

My Dearest Darling.

I have only received one airgraph-er-letter I mean
from you for a long time but as it was a very
important one I think it warrants a reply by sea-mail
as I have more space whereon to write.

. . .

Now about this idea of yours you suggest that
after this war we move to South Africa and make a
permanent home there. One thing that looms
foremost in my mind. What occupation would you
contemplate taking on arrival there, do you think you
could or would look out for something on the same
lines as you were doing before you joined up? Oh
heck? whats the use of trying to be practical and help-
ful when I am so excited with the whole idea that I
find it difficult to write at all. I love the suggestion,
even when you say I should be parted from my
people may be for years I get a nasty jolt admittedly,
but it soon wears off when I think of the advantages
to this scheme. After all we cannot live tied to our
parents apron strings all our lives even though I have
not strayed far from them in the last 20 years. The
part about South Africa being further away from
Europe in the event of another war cuts both ways.

Should our children get any crazy patriotic ideas and desire to join up, they would have to go further from us, but there again they may not get these crazy ideas. How do you mean there is no unemployment like England, what do folks do when they are fired is it so easy to obtain a position that there is no need for a dole scheme. One thing you say – better wages, that means the cost of living must be higher so should anything happen that you found it impossible to get a job etc. we should have a pretty hard time of it. I must get some library books and read up about Suid Afrique a bit. To put my views in a nutshell I am thrilled pink, and we must fight tooth and nail not to let this scheme fall through.

Talking of Africa and teeth and claws etc reminds me I have just been reading some Tarzan books. The return of Tarzan, and Son of Tarzan to be exact and I loved them I must try and get some more a bit of light reading does not hurt any-one especially as I have just finished some very heavy stuff, perhaps it was just the reaction from said heavy stuff that made me enjoy Tarzan so much, any how I must read the others, as soon as I can.

. . .

I cannot get any alchohol for my perfume, I have tried at several Carlislian and Dumfriesian chemists for 20 grammes of pure alchohol without success so I guess I'll have to wait until after the war before I can stink the place out with my exotic (not erotic) perfume. I hope the war does not last long as I want to try it out and see how many swooning he men I can capture.

Eric and Sheila, Anthony and Carol, Stephen and Christine and Paul and Alayne send their love and all hope Daddy will come home soon complete with camels, sphinxes, pyramids and all the various other junk that they have asked for. I want you home too Darling but not because I want any c's s's or p's. I just want you repeat *YOU*.

Well this is the longest letter I have written to you for a long time isn't it, several pages usually gets me by the short hairs these days but here I am on my sixth large sheet and still going strong. I must have been brought up on Johnny Walker.

Do you realise I am now 20 years and 5 months old and that soon I shall have come of age and get the front door key. If you come home soon I can get married regardless of parental arguments. Then we'll show the world what we can do in the family line. I want at least eight. Eight little South Africans can you imagine it. Me with eight bouncing wee brats and you trying hard to foot the bills.

Oh Well Darling I can't write any more as this is my last sheet of paper and the only other stuff I have handy is an RAF message form.

Bye Bye for now.

I'll always love you

Betty

GLOSSARY

ACCS	Accumulators
AD	After duty
AIRGRAPH	A one sheet letter which was microfilmed and printed out at destination
CHIEFY	Flight Sergeant
GEN	Information
GROUPY	Group Captain
IC	In charge
LAC	Leading Aircraftsman
LACW	Leading Aircraftswoman
LPTB	London Transport Passenger Board (bus requisitioned by RAF)
NAAFI	Navy Army and Airforce Institution
PROPS	Badge of rank of LAC or LACW
RAFVR	Royal Air Force Volunteer Reserve
RTO	Radio Telegraphy Operator
SOP	Sleeping out pass
SPARKS	Trade badge of RTO
SPS	RAF Special Police
SSQ	Station sick quarters
TOPS	As RTO
WAAF	Womens Auxiliary Air Force
WADS	Rock Cakes
1250	Identity card with photo carried by all ranks